WHERE
THEY
FELL

WHERE THEY FELL

A WALKER'S GUIDE
TO THE BATTLEFIELDS
OF THE WORLD

TIM NEWARK

A QUARTO BOOK

First edition for the United States, its territories and dependencies and Canada published in 2000 by Barron's Educational Series, Inc.

All inquiries should be addressed to
Barron's Educational Series, Inc.
250 Wireless Boulevard
Hauppauge, NY 11788
http://www.barronseduc.com

Library of Congress Catalog Card No: 99-069496

ISBN 0-7641-5247-5

QUAR.WKTB

Conceived, designed, and produced by Quarto Publishing plc
The Old Brewery
6 Blundell Street
London
N7 9BH

Editor KATE MICHELL   *Art editor* ELIZABETH HEALEY
Text editors MARY SENECHAL,   *Designer* MALCOLM SMYTHE
          PETER KIRKHAM   *Photographer* IAN HOWES
Indexer DOROTHY FRAME   *Cartographer* MALCOLM SWANSTON

Art Director MOIRA CLINCH   *Publisher* PIERS SPENCE

Manufactured in China by Regent Publishing services, Limited
Printed in China by Midas Printing Limited

987654321

CONTENTS

THE SOIL
OF BATTLE

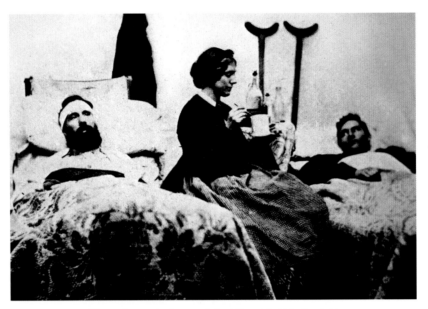

Above, *A nurse tends wounded soldiers* *at the Union hospital in Nashville, Tennessee. The great number of casualties during the American Civil War encouraged the nation to honor its dead and wounded soldiers.*

Left, *Visitors to the battlefield at Antietam* *walk along the fortified sunken road known as Bloody Lane, where so many Confederate and Union soldiers lost their lives.*

BATTLEFIELDS ARE SACRED LAND. Before the decision was made to respect the bodies of those who perished in battle, and remove them to a national cemetery where their families could mourn them, the dead and wounded were left where they fell. It was the great battles such as Gettysburg, in which thousands died for their beliefs in country and freedom, that persuaded public figures to celebrate the sacrifice enacted on the field of combat. The Gettysburg Address of United States President Abraham Lincoln in 1863 marked a significant moment in the linking of battle with political liberty. It recognized that the soldiers who died for a nation's ambitions were special people, deserving of lasting respect. "From these honored dead," Lincoln declared, "we take increased devotion to that cause for which they gave the last full measure of devotion; that we here highly resolve that these dead shall not have died in vain."

Until that time the "common soldier" had been largely regarded as a troublesome, underclass tool to be used by generals. He ceased to be of interest when he died, except to the scavengers who stripped and looted dead bodies on the battlefield. If he was lucky, he might be thrown into a large, unmarked mass grave; otherwise his body would be left to rot where it lay. Even in the twentieth century, the magnitude of destruction wrought on some battlefields—especially on the Western Front during World War I—meant that not all bodies could be recovered. Most of the battlefields described in this book are, in effect, unmarked cemeteries. A sense of quiet respect is appropriate when walking these hallowed grounds.

THE GEOGRAPHY OF WAR

To walk a battlefield is more than an act of homage to past sacrifice, it also an act of historical exploration. It is one thing to read firsthand accounts of battle; it is another to visit the site. There, you can fully understand the challenges of a battle, the physical obstacles faced by the soldiers and their generals. You can also gain an insight into the accidents of nature that led great warlords, such as Napoleon and Hitler, to make the mistakes that led to their downfalls.

The tragic scenario of World War I—soldiers mired in waterlogged trenches over a period of years—was determined largely by the geography of the landscape. The Third Battle of Ypres (or Passchendaele) was fought across the Flanders plain, which is composed mostly of blue clay. This is a sticky, dense soil impervious to water, so that rain accumulates in pools on its surface. This is good news for farmers who use the pools to irrigate their fields; but when canals are destroyed by shelling, and water gathers in myriad bomb craters, the landscape is transformed into a sea of mud, bog-

Above, "General Frost shaving Little Boney": a caricature of 1812, showing Napoleon being defeated in Russia by the weather. Despite being a master of command on the battlefield, Napoleon sometimes paid too little attention to geography and weather, which resulted in defeat.

ging down any military advances and condemning soldiers to a living hell of filth and damp. Farther south, in the Somme region, the land is mainly chalk. Rain drains through this porous stone, so that trenches could be dug more easily and mines pushed under enemy lines. The great mines that exploded at the beginning of the Battle of the Somme were possible here, whereas mining around Ypres was a much more difficult enterprise. Military geologists soon became important to warfare on the Western Front.

The weeks of heavy rain did not help the British and their allies at Passchendaele. A similar lack of good weather contributed to Napoleon's downfall at Waterloo—also fought in Belgian mud. Heavy rain the night before the battle meant that Napoleon was

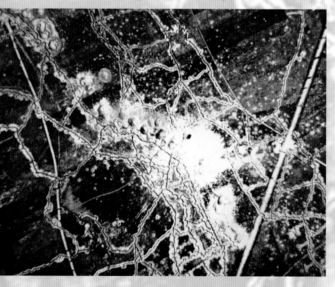

Above, Aerial photograph showing the mass of shell craters inflicted on a section of the Western Front during World War I. Enormous damage, such as this, to the landscape, created a sea of mud in which soldiers drowned and advances ground to a halt.

forced to delay his attack against the Allied lines until noon, and when it did come its impact was lessened by the deadening effect on men and horses of an advance through thick, waterlogged clay. My own visit to Waterloo was bedeviled by a heavy downpour, and there is something especially demoralizing about trudging across clinging mud that makes the physical effort of walking even more arduous, in addition to ruining one's clothes and equipment.

At Waterloo, Napoleon attacked regardless of the landscape. He believed that his generalship was superior to the limitations of geography—his spirit would overcome everything. His opponent the Duke of Wellington, however, was a past master at using the landscape. At Waterloo, Wellington hid the majority of his troops behind the ridge that ran across the battlefield. This helped to protect his men from artillery fire, and to disguise the strength of his formations from the enemy. He also used local features, such as farms and sunken roads, to anchor his defensive position.

During the American Civil War, Confederate General Robert E. Lee embraced local defensive features to brilliant effect at the Battle of Antietam. His use of the sunken road known as Bloody Lane enabled him to defeat a larger force—at least until the Union troops managed to flank and enfilade the position, turning it into a Confederate death trap. Unfortunately, this lesson did not influence him at Gettysburg, where he adopted a more Napoleonic faith in attack, and saw his men throw themselves vainly against defensive positions formed by hills and fences. Lee was both served and undone by the ground on which he fought.

Above, *General Robert E. Lee* was one of the greatest Confederate generals of the American Civil War.

Adolf Hitler, the supreme commander of the German Army during World War II, understood the advantages of weather and landscape, but allowed his total confidence in victory to carry him beyond the success he could realistically expect. The Battle of the Bulge was a brilliantly conceived final assault against the Allies in western Europe. Hitler achieved surprise by sending his armored divisions through the narrow roads and dense forest of the Ardennes. By attacking in the winter, he took advantage of poor weather to help shield his forces from Allied air attacks. But the offensive pushed ahead too far, stretching its supply lines to breaking point. Bastogne, in the center of the bulge, became a focus of American resistance, and the same bad weather hindered the

Above, *Adolf Hitler, supreme commander of the German army* during World War II, takes time out to view Paris after having rapidly defeated the French army. Hitler's blitzkreig successes made him overconfident and, like Napoleon, he underestimated the impact of weather and geography on future campaigns, which contributed to his defeat.

Above, *The Newfoundland Memorial Park*
commemorates the 1st Newfoundland Regiment, which was virtually annihilated in the Battle of the Somme.

troops of both sides. When the skies finally cleared and Allied aircraft could fly again, Hitler's last gamble was doomed.

The British at Gallipoli in World War I were undone by a combination of local geography and climate. The sparse hilly land around the coast of the Turkish peninsula made any advance against a well-entrenched enemy impossible, and when the Allies found themselves pinned down by bullets, the relentless heat of the Mediterranean sun achieved the rest, eventually forcing the Allies to leave after months of fruitless fighting.

At Normandy in 1944, the Allied D-Day landings were remarkable for their thorough preparation and understanding of both the land and the weather. The result was a generally effective landing at several points, which, combined with air superiority, gave the Germans, whom the Allies had deceived into concentrating around Calais, little time to respond to the rapid advance inland.

LAYERS OF TIME

A battle traumatizes both people and landscape. But whereas monuments and history books commemorate the human destruction long after personal memories fade, the damage wrought on nature is quickly covered by new growth. The poppy—an abiding emblem of the loss of life in World War I—is symbolic of nature's renewal; its beautiful red flowers rapidly carpeted the churned-up mud of the Western Front. Trees grow over ravaged land, and at the heavily wooded Civil War battle-fields of Shiloh and Antietam it is difficult now to appreciate fully the blasted landscape across which the soldiers fought. Yet these locations are imbued with an eerie beauty.

The effects of passing time are even more intriguing when the battle was fought in an urban environment. Sometimes the locations are preserved as monuments symbolic of the fight for freedom, such as the Alamo in San Antonio. At Louisbourg, part of the old French fortress was reconstructed at great expense as an expression of pride in the French cultural heritage of Canada. At Bunker Hill in Boston, a simple obelisk expresses the moment when revolutionaries defied

Above, *A U.S. soldier inspects a damaged German Panzerjäger,*
("tank hunter")—an 88mm self-propelled gun on a Panther tank chassis—destroyed during the breakout campaign following the successful landings at Normandy in 1944. Mechanized vehicles, such as tanks, enabled battlefields to spread over far wider areas than in the conflicts of previous centuries.

an empire. At Pearl Harbor, the U.S. Navy recognizes the destruction wrought there, but also puts it in context, and the area continues as a working harbor. Life goes on—and a victorious peace is attained by overcoming the damage of the past. The Belgian town of Ypres was rebuilt exactly as it had been before its destruction by the German army in World War I, as a national act of defiance and rebirth.

THROUGH GENERALS' EYES

As you walk across a battlefield, it is instructive to view it through a general's eyes. Military commanders used soldiers as scouts to assess the land ahead. Before the advent of mechanized warfare in the twentieth century, these were light cavalrymen who had several tasks to achieve. They were raiders, grabbing loot for themselves and finding food and supplies for the army, while terrifying the civilian population into submission.

Above, *View of the Tennessee River.* *Control of the river proved crucial during the Battle of Shiloh, allowing the Union forces to receive reinforcements and survive the Confederate onslaught.*

In addition, they were the eyes and ears of their commanders, reporting back on the shape of the landscape and its major features, as well as looking out for the enemy and estimating the size of opposing forces. Sometimes the scouts became embroiled in skirmishes with the enemy that then turned into major battles. At Gettysburg, for example, two advance units clashed with each other in the town, which encouraged their commanders to concentrate their troops for a battle.

The first aspect of the landscape that past commanders sought was high ground. Possession of this feature provided several advantages. It enabled the high-ground troops to see the enemy. It also meant that either the enemy must attack uphill, which is exhausting, or that the high-ground forces could charge downhill. The Battle of Hastings was a classic occasion when the defending Saxons chose a perfect steep ridge for their position. Unfortunately, it did not prevent their defeat by a relentless foe.

A second aspect was the location of water. This could indicate boggy ground that would be difficult to cross. It could make a useful defensive position, covering a flank to slow and confuse the enemy. A river could also facilitate delivery of crucial supplies and reinforcements, as at the Battle of Shiloh.

The quality of the ground was important. Would it be easy to dig trenches and thus create a strong defensive position; or was the terrain stony, providing a clear target platform for the enemy? Trees and thick vegetation were difficult to traverse, but could provide excellent cover from which to surprise the enemy. Farms and villages could be turned into fortresses.

All these aspects of geography flowed through the mind of a good commander. The following battlefield tour maps give you the opportunity to make your own decisions and judge the wisdom of past commanders' choices.

Above, *A pyramid of cannon balls on Shiloh's battlefield* *marks the site of the Union headquarters of General W. H. L. Wallace. Out of five Union divisional camps at Shiloh, Wallace's headquarters were the only ones to escape capture by the Confederates at the beginning of the battle.*

NORTH AMERICA

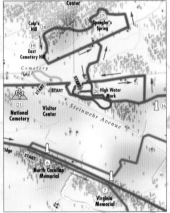

The fight for freedom has never been more fiercely fought than in North America.

From the forests of Canada to the desert of Texas, the landscape of the battlefield is a testament to the relentless struggle for independence.

They began as battles against empires and culminated in the test of civil war in which two ways of life clashed.

The battles of the American Civil War resulted in tremendous sacrifice on both sides and a determination never to repeat such horror on American soil.

PRIDE OF FRANCE

Above, ***Colonel James Wolfe***—*later the hero of the capture of Quebec—
bravely leads ashore a brigade of soldiers in the assault on Louisbourg.*

Left, ***An attendant in period costume stands guard over the Dauphin Gate,***
the entrance to Louisbourg fortress, as a French soldier would have done in 1758.

BACKGROUND TO BATTLE

The Seven Years' War (1756-63) has been called the first world war, because the colonial super-powers, Britain and France, fought around the globe over each other's colonies.

The North American phase of this struggle—the French and Indian War—began two years earlier in 1754. It was fought primarily over the forts that controlled trade in the region.

The fortress of Louisbourg was crucial to the control of New France in Canada, and the British had already assaulted it unsuccessfully in 1745.

In 1754, fighting broke out between French and English colonists in Canada. Reinforcements of soldiers and experienced generals arrived on both sides. The Marquis de Montcalm-Gozon, the French commander, inflicted several defeats against the British.

In June 1757, a British expedition was sent against Louisbourg, but the fleet was scattered by a storm and the expedition was abandoned.

In the fall of 1757, a decision was made in London to eliminate France once and for all from North America—a concerted effort was planned for the capture of Louisbourg the following year.

L OUISBOURG WAS THE PRIDE OF FRANCE. Soon after the French settled around the Gulf of St. Lawrence in southeastern Canada in 1713, the small fishing port began to emerge as one of the key commercial centers of the New World. Construction started on a massive fortress to guard Louisbourg's ice-free harbor and hugely profitable cod-fishing industry. It took so long to build, and cost so much—over $200 million in today's money—that King Louis XV said he expected to be able to see the fortress from across the Atlantic in France. On its completion, the fortress was the largest building in North America.

The circuit walls of the Louisbourg fortress were over one and a half miles long. Inside were 4,000 civilians, 4,000 regular French troops, 220 cannons, some marines and militia, friendly Indians, and 3,000 sailors. This was a population almost as large as that of all the other French Canadian settlements combined. There were also 12 French men o'war in the harbor. But the fortress had its weaknesses. It had been built on boggy marshland, and corrupt French officials had turned a blind eye to inferior construction. As a result, the mortar in the masonry was of poor quality, and the massive walls were beginning to crumble.

WAR OF FORTS

When France and Britain went to war over their colonies in North America, their forts were prime objectives, because they guarded strategically important areas and provided gateways to the wealth of the continent. Louisbourg was high on the British list of targets, and in 1758 a British fleet sailed toward the awesome fortress. Major General Jeffrey Amherst commanded the forces, which

numbered some 9,000 British troops, including Highlanders, along with 500 colonial volunteers. With him sailed a young colonel named James Wolfe—later to become the most famous British commander in the New World.

In early June 1758, the British fleet arrived off the Canadian coast. The shore was rocky and the sea was rough, making it difficult to disembark the troops. Amherst reconnoitered all of the possible landing locations, and chose Freshwater Cove, at the mouth of a river, as an especially sheltered area. This position would enable him to attack the fortress from the rear, instead of confronting its formidable front, and his ships could cover the assault.

Storms and fog frustrated the landings for five days. Eventually, on June 8, Wolfe led a brigade toward the shore. Other brigades landed elsewhere to distract the French, but a body of French soldiers were entrenched just above Wolfe's intended landing point

*Below, **British soldiers clamber aboard rowing boats** to attack Louisbourg during an earlier expedition against the formidable French fortress.*

NO SAFE HAVEN

Louisbourg was subjected to a fierce bombardment by British artillery for over a month. Captain John Knox witnessed its effect on the defenders, both civilians and soldiers:

> The Citadel was soon demolished by fire from the batteries. I saw flames for several hours. A small number of casemates, or rooms in the thickness of the fortress walls of the King's Bastion, are used to shut up the Ladies and part of the women of the town: one casemate is assigned to the wounded officers.
> All the women with a considerable number of little children came out, running hither and thither, not knowing where to go in the midst of the bombs and the bullets, that were falling on every side: also several officers, sick and wounded, were carried on stretchers, without a safe haven, in which they could be placed.

From AN HISTORICAL JOURNAL OF THE CAMPAIGNS IN NORTH AMERICA *by Captain John Knox (1769).*

Today, drummers of the Compagnie Franche de la Marine recreate the atmosphere of battle outside the Guardhouse at the King's Bastion.

Left, *An Iroquois warrior,*
with a scalp on his musket barrel. Indian warriors fought alongside both the British and the French in the war for control of North America. Taking scalps was a standard feature of battle to Indian warriors.

and they opened heavy fire. Wolfe made an immediate decision to withdraw, but some of his men had already landed, so he changed his mind and gathered his troops beneath the shelter of a cliff. With bayonets fixed, the British then stormed the French trenches, and the rest of the British army was able to land safely.

PINEAPPLES AND CHAMPAGNE

Amherst pitched his camp just beyond the range of the guns of Louisbourg. His cannons silenced the guns that sought to prevent his ships from entering the shelter of the harbor, and the French ships now huddled beneath the walls of the fortress. Thousands of British soldiers labored to dig earthworks nearer and nearer to the French fortress, so that their guns could blast away at it. The weakness in the masonry began to tell, and both French civilians and soldiers suffered in the bombardment. The French sent out groups of soldiers to attack the British as they dug their earthworks. The British counterattacked by hurling shells at the French ships anchored in Louisbourg harbor. One lucky shot struck the powder magazine of a ship, exploding it in a ball

Above, *General Jeffrey Amherst,* *commander of the British expedition against Louisbourg in 1758.*

Below, *The restored governor's chapel* *and apartments in the King's Bastion.*

of flames and setting fire to adjacent vessels. With a quarter of their number sick and injured in the hospital, the defenders were nearing exhaustion.

Amid the suffering, however, the two commanders were waging a contest of compliments. To raise the morale of the French troops, the governor's wife fired three cannons at the enemy. Amherst responded by sending her two pineapples freshly arrived from the Azores. Madame replied with a crate of champagne, and Amherst sent her two more pineapples and a firkin of butter. But gallant gestures could not save the fortress. On July 26, the French governor surrendered. One thousand French soldiers lay dead within the ruined walls.

LOUISBOURG

STANDING ON THE reconstructed land-ward walls of Louisbourg fortress, one can look across the countryside and imagine an eighteenth-century siege in progress. Rows of trenches slowly move toward the walls as British soldiers dig, knowing this battle will be won more by the spade than the musket. Cannons are hauled into place on newly dug mounds of earth, and the nearer they get to the walls, the more damage they inflict.

By the mid-eighteenth century, artillery had become increasingly effective, and many regarded it as the battle-winning element of an army. The British at Louisbourg had three main types of cannon: 3-pounders, 6-pounders, and 12-pounders, named for the weight of the solid-iron cannonballs they fired. They also had howitzers: artillery that fired exploding shells in a high arc, so that they landed behind the walls of the

A recreated British redcoat of the Coldstream Regiment of Foot Guards—typical of the soldiers who fought in the French and Indian War.

French town, blowing homes apart and starting fires. It must have been a terrifying experience for the civilian population.

"There is not a house in the place that has not felt the effects of this formidable artillery," recorded one French officer. "From yesterday morning till seven o'clock this evening, we reckon that a thousand, or twelve hundred, bombs, great and small, have been thrown into the town, accompanied all the time by the fire of forty pieces of cannon."

It was not only the French who were fearful. Before the British had established their positions, they lived in constant terror of attack by Indians. Several British soldiers were captured at an early stage, and one of the few who escaped reported the belief that the Indians intended to roast their prisoners alive. Tales of scalping and torture added to the British soldiers' fear as they set up their camp.

PLAN OF BATTLE

Louisbourg, on Isle Royale (now Cape Breton), was surrounded by rocky shores and rough seas. It was a very difficult place to assault by an amphibious landing, and the British nearly lost the battle on the beaches at Freshwater Cove. It was only a French lack of nerve—they failed to put up a strong resistance and retreated to the fortress—that allowed Wolfe's brigade ashore. The brigade then set up camp to the rear of the fortress. It remained for the British artillery to reduce the mighty bastion to ruins.

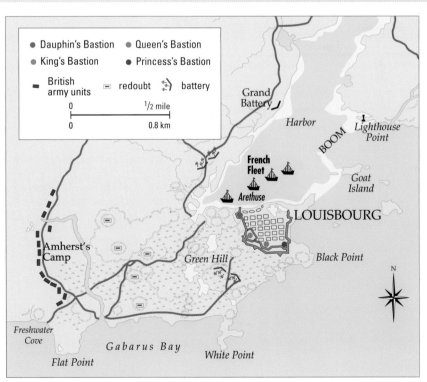

- Dauphin's Bastion
- Queen's Bastion
- King's Bastion
- Princess's Bastion
- British army units
- redoubt
- battery

0 ————— 1/2 mile
0 ————— 0.8 km

Grand Battery

Harbor

BOOM

Lighthouse Point

French Fleet

Goat Island

Arethuse

LOUISBOURG

Amherst's Camp

Green Hill

Black Point

N

Freshwater Cove

Gabarus Bay

White Point

Flat Point

LOUISBOURG

ONCE THE GREAT FORTRESS OF NEW FRANCE, guarding the Gulf of St. Lawrence and the approach to Quebec, Louisbourg was left in ruins by the British. Today it is rising again, in a huge reconstruction project. One-quarter of the fortress and its landward fortifications are being rebuilt according to the original plans. Inside, you can visit authentic eighteenth-century homes, taverns, and barracks, and actors recreate the lifestyle of New France.

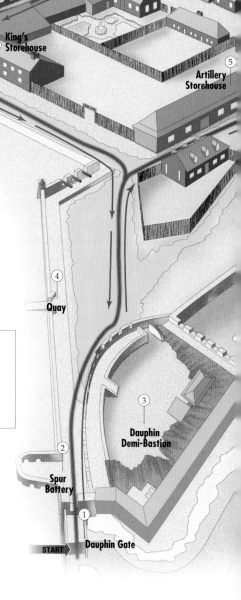

Above, **"Residents" in period costume** repair a house in Louisbourg, using original methods and materials.

QUAY

French warships took shelter at the quay (4) that runs alongside the harbor, where they were set on fire by a British shell.

Key

(3)   Battlefield tour stop

START   Starting point

    Battlefield tour route

Above, **Firing a cannon from the Spur Battery (2)** overlooking the harbor during a reenactment of the attack on Louisbourg.

DAUPHIN GATE

Once you have passed through the Dauphin Gate (1) into Louisbourg fortress, you step back in time to the eighteenth century .

MUSEUM

The museum (9) displays a scale model of the fortress and some of the site's earliest artifacts. It is also the beginning of a walk through the eighteenth-century ruins.

KING'S BASTION

The King's Bastion (7) is a fortress within a fortress. It formed part of the formidable fortifications facing the British bombardment. The governor's apartments, officers' quarters, and soldiers' barracks have all been restored.

GETTING THERE

LOCATION: Cape Breton Island, Nova Scotia, Canada.

VISITOR INFORMATION: Fortress of Louisbourg National Historic Site. P.O. Box 160, Louisbourg, Nova Scotia, B0A 1M0.

TELEPHONE: 902-733-2280

DIRECTIONS: 23 miles (37 km) south of Sydney, Cape Breton, on Route 22, just beyond modern town of Louisbourg. Take exit 8 near Sydney.

TOUR DISTANCE: 2½ miles (4 km).

LOUISBOURG

⑧ Guardhouse

⑦ King's Bastion

King's Battery

Above, **The King's Bastion area of the fort (7),** as the British would have seen it in 1758, showing the mounds of earth raised around the fortress to protect it from bombardment.

Left, **The restoration of a typical street** inside the Louisbourg fortifications shows the wood and stone houses of the mid-eighteenth century.

DAUPHIN DEMI-BASTION

The artillery battery, barracks, and powder magazine are recreated at the Dauphin Demi-Bastion (3).

DEFYING AN EMPIRE

Above, *Soldiers of the American Continental Army*—the revolutionaries—at target practice. (Painting by H.A. Ogden.)

Left, *Modern-day Boston* is a charming city that retains many buildings of a previous age, such as those on Beacon Hill. Follow the Freedom Trail to visit all the city sites associated with the American Revolution.

B Y THE LATE EIGHTEENTH CENTURY, the British Empire was a formidable global power. It had battled three of its principal European rivals—the Netherlands, Spain, and France—and defeated them all. The seas of the world were its highways, and its influence stretched from the ports of India to the forests of North America. None of this, however, deterred the American colonists, who made their first military bid for independence in 1775. At the Battle of Bunker Hill they faced the military might of the British Empire, to surprising effect.

BOSTON BESIEGED

Following the first shots of the War for American Independence at Lexington Common in April 1775, a patriot militia of 15,000 men laid siege to the British garrison in Boston. Boston lies on a peninsula, and the British commander and Governor of Massachusetts, General Thomas Gage, had fortified its narrow causeway, Boston Neck, the previous year. But he had not secured the high ground that overlooked Boston from across the water: the two peninsulas known as the

BACKGROUND TO BATTLE

The American War of Independence began in April 1775 when the British General Thomas Gage marched with troops to Concord to capture a store of arms and ammunition amassed by the colonists.

Paul Revere of Boston rode through the night to alert the revolutionaries, and they met the British with a company of 70 men on Lexington Common on April 19. British soldiers fired a volley and the Americans dispersed, but more gathered to confront the Redcoats at Concord Bridge, and, as the British retired, the colonists harassed the column all the way back to Boston, inflicting almost 300 casualties.

The Massachusetts Provincial Congress raised a militia army and put Boston under siege.

On June 15, the Second Continental Congress in Philadelphia designated the forces besieging Boston a Continental Army, ordered the addition of six companies of riflemen, and raised Colonel George Washington of Virginia to the rank of general and overall commander.

Right, British troops surge over the American defenses to fight hand-to-hand with the colonists still holding the position. (Painting by H. Charles McBarron.)

Below, A handbill distributed among troops loyal to the British encouraging them to desert is an early example of wartime propaganda .

Charlestown Heights and the Dorchester Heights. During May, British reinforcements sailed into Boston harbor, bringing the strength of the British garrison to 8,000. With them were three generals: William Howe, Henry Clinton, and John Burgoyne. They decided to break out from Boston, but word reached the Americans, and they moved first. They occupied Bunker Hill on the Charlestown Heights, the peninsula that overlooks the north side of Boston.

The American commander on the Charlestown Heights was Colonel William Prescott, a farmer with experience of fighting from the French and Indian War (1754–1763). On the evening of June 16, Prescott led between 1,200 and 1,500 men out of Cambridge onto the Charlestown peninsula. Instead of remaining on Bunker Hill, Prescott ordered his men to dig in on the lower prominence of Breed's Hill. By the following day, they had created a fortified

PROSPECT HILL.	BUNKER's HILL.
I. Seven Dollars a Month.	I. Three Pence a Day.
II. Fresh Provisions, and in Plenty.	II. Rotten Salt Pork.
III. Health.	III. The Scurvy.
IV. Freedom, Ease, Affluence and a good Farm.	IV. Slavery, Beggary and Want.

HANDBILL I

position with a redoubt about 45 yards long that was linked by a breastwork to an existing hedge and stone wall. The work was so exhausting that some volunteers abandoned the operation and disappeared.

REBEL FIREPOWER

The British sailed across Boston harbor in barges and landed on the northeast corner of Charlestown, at Morton's Point. The landing was covered by fire from three British warships: *Falcon*, *Lively*, and *Somerset*. Howe was in command of over 2,500 regular British troops, including grenadiers, light infantry, and foot regiments. One of the generals suggested sending another force to attack the rear of the American position, but Gage was confident enough to order a frontal assault. It was a hot June afternoon as the first wave of redcoats marched up Breed's Hill. They came under strong fire from flanking troops placed in the settlement of

PRELUDE TO BUNKER HILL

An indication of the determined resistance the British Army in Boston would face at Bunker Hill was revealed during their earlier raid on Concord. A soldier in the British Light Infantry recorded his view of combat with the Rebels in a letter to his family, revealing the sense of surprise at their firepower:

On a hill near Concord there was assembled a number of people [Rebel militia], about 700, at exercise; they were ready prepared for us, being all loaded with powder and ball. We then halted, and looked at them, as cocks might do on a pit before they fight. But it was not our business to wait long looking at them; so we fixed our bayonets, and immediately charged them up the hill, in order to disperse them; but we were greatly mistaken; for they were not to be dispersed so easily, the whole of them giving us a smart fire . . . . [After Concord, the Rebels] fired so constantly from the hills, the back of stone walls, and out of the houses, so smart upon us, that we were glad to retreat as fast as possible to Boston.

Quoted *in* LETTERS ON THE AMERICAN REVOLUTION, *edited by Margaret Willard (Published in Boston, 1825).*

A contemporary painting depicts British artillery in Boston and British men o'war in the Charles River bombarding Charlestown and setting it on fire. British troops are shown advancing up Breed's Hill toward the American positions.

Charlestown. Burgoyne directed his artillery fire at the settlement, and it went up in flames, but the British assault faltered. The British were too far away when they fired, whereas the Americans held their fire until the combination of bullets and buckshot at close range would be fatal. Unable to respond effectively, the British fell back.

The British re-formed at the base of the hill, but many of their officers were injured, and when the troops advanced again, they met the same hail of fire. Howe bravely led both assaults in person, but the second time he found himself almost alone in command, as most of his officers had been killed. The Americans were jubilant, but their ammunition was running low. Howe knew that any additional delay would cause the complete collapse of his soldiers' morale, and he

Above, *Statue of Paul Revere,* the Bostonian who rode all night to warn the colonists that the British Army was advancing toward Concord.

rallied them for a third attack. With 500 fresh reinforcements, Howe surged up the hill again. This time, American firepower was less decisive, and the redcoats took the hill with their bayonets. The Americans fought a tough rear-guard action, but the battle was over. The British had won, but the Americans had proved that they could take on the forces of an empire, and might, but for a lack of ammunition, have beaten them. The British lost 42 percent of their attacking force, including 24 officers and 202 soldiers killed, and 828 wounded. The Americans suffered less than half that figure in casualties: 140 dead, 271 wounded, and 30 taken prisoner.

On July 23, American General George Washington arrived at Boston to continue the siege against the British.

Below, Boston Harbor today; skyscrapers and the Bunker Hill Pavilion dominate the view from the Charles River. In 1775, the river was commanded by British warships.

BUNKER HILL

Boston contains many monuments relating to the American Revolution and to the events that formed the background to the battle. One reason why the colonists felt bold enough to face the mighty British redcoats in open battle at Bunker Hill was their previous triumph at Concord on April 19.

The British were demoralized by this American success, as is expressed in one British soldier's report: "On our leaving Concord to return to Boston, they began to fire on us from behind walls, ditches, trees, etc., which, as we marched, increased to a very great degree, and continued without intermission

Above, The Hannah, *the first battleship of the American Navy, was commissioned in the year of Bunker Hill to combat the enormous sea power of the British. (Painting by Van Howell.)*

of five minutes altogether, for, I believe, upwards of eighteen miles."

The firing did not stop until the British reached Bunker Hill in Charlestown, where they were protected by British battleships anchored in the Charles River.

In this rehearsal for the conflict at Bunker Hill, the British suffered 247 casualties and 26 missing. The Americans suffered 93 casulaties. News of this savaging spread like wildfire among the revolutionaries. Soon afterward, 15,000 Americans laid siege to Boston, and the psychological background to the Battle of Bunker Hill was established—the Americans would not be unnerved by ranks of imperial redcoats.

PLAN OF BATTLE

This map shows Charlestown peninsula, to the north of Boston Harbor. Over 2,000 British troops, commanded by General Howe, landed at Morton's Point, covered by cannon fire from British warships and gunboats. Colonel Prescott's 1,200 or more American patriots occupied Breed's Hill, and defenses ran all the way to the Mystic River. They also occupied the settlement of Charlestown, from where they offered flanking fire until they were eliminated by British artillery. British reinforcements landed farther south.

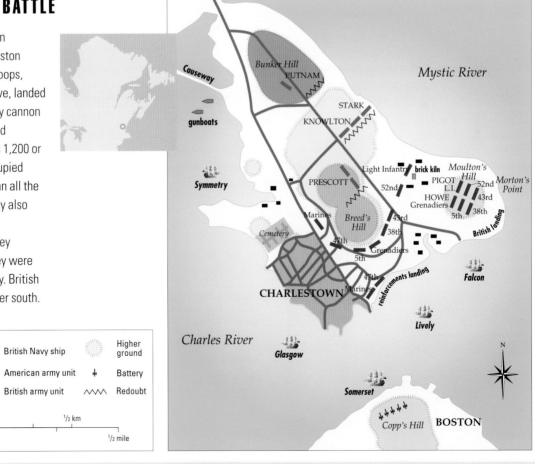

🚢 British Navy ship	⬡	Higher ground
▬ American army unit	⚓	Battery
▬ British army unit	∧∧∧	Redoubt

0 ———— ½ km
0 ———————————— ½ mile

BUNKER HILL

UNKER HILL IN CHARLESTOWN is now part of the sophisticated urban sprawl of Boston. The water once navigated by eighteenth-century battleships is land, and the Charles River is reduced to little more than a basin, with bridges across it to downtown Boston.

GETTING THERE

LOCATION:

Boston, Massachusetts.

VISITOR INFORMATION:

Boston National Historical Park, Charlestown Navy Yard, Boston, MA 02129-4543.

TELEPHONE:

617-242-5641

DIRECTIONS: *About half a mile (0.8 km) from downtown Boston, across Charlestown Bridge into Charlestown, on Route 1 off I-93.*

TOUR DISTANCE:

1½ miles (3 km).

Left, British redcoats advance into withering American fire delivered from the colonists' defensive position on top of Breed's Hill. (Painting by Howard Pyle.)

THE CHARLES RIVER

Three British battleships on the Charles River bombarded American defenses on Breed's Hill to cover the British landing.

Charles River Dam

Charles River

Charles River

Charlesbank Park

WEST END

Cambridge Street

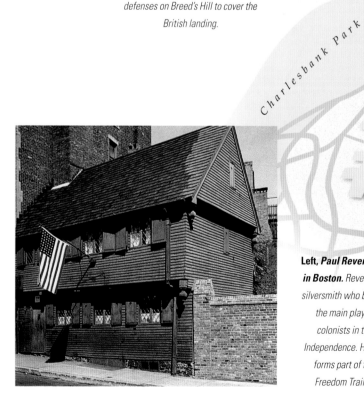

Left, Paul Revere's House (1) in Boston. Revere was a local silversmith who became one of the main players for the colonists in the War of Independence. His house now forms part of the historic Freedom Trail in Boston.

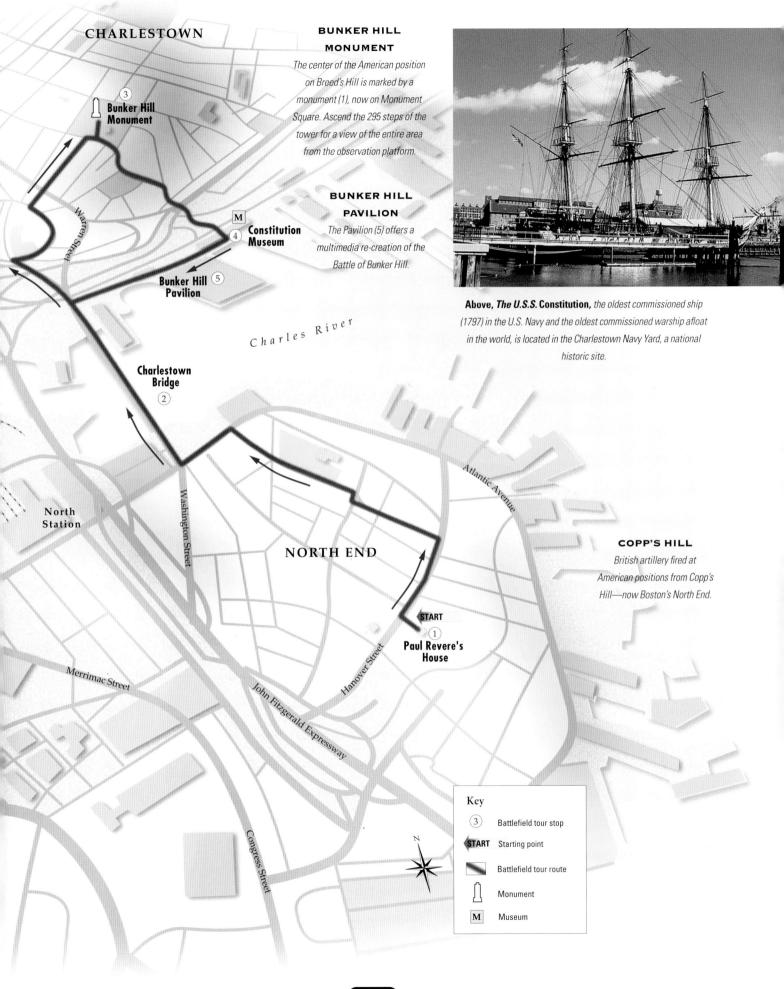

CHARLESTOWN

BUNKER HILL MONUMENT

The center of the American position on Breed's Hill is marked by a monument (1), now on Monument Square. Ascend the 295 steps of the tower for a view of the entire area from the observation platform.

③ Bunker Hill Monument

Ⓜ
④ **Constitution Museum**

BUNKER HILL PAVILION

The Pavilion (5) offers a multimedia re-creation of the Battle of Bunker Hill.

Bunker Hill Pavilion ⑤

Charles River

Above, The U.S.S. Constitution, *the oldest commissioned ship (1797) in the U.S. Navy and the oldest commissioned warship afloat in the world, is located in the Charlestown Navy Yard, a national historic site.*

Charlestown Bridge
②

Warren Street

Washington Street

Atlantic Avenue

North Station

NORTH END

COPP'S HILL

British artillery fired at American positions from Copp's Hill—now Boston's North End.

START
①
Paul Revere's House

Hanover Street

Merrimac Street

John Fitzgerald Expressway

Congress Street

N

Key

③ Battlefield tour stop

START Starting point

Battlefield tour route

Monument

Ⓜ Museum

NEVER SURRENDER

Above, *Frontiersman Davy Crockett,* who died fighting for Texas at the Battle of the Alamo.

Left, *The pretty River Walk* alongside the San Antonio River is the modern face of the city of the same name. At the city's heart stands the monument to the bitter fighting for control of Texas—the Alamo.

ACCORDING TO GENERAL ANTONIO LOPEZ DE SANTA ANNA, the siege of the Alamo was "but a small affair." In numbers of combatants, this was true. Only 188 Texans fought against almost 4,000 Mexicans, but the stand the Texans took has inspired generations of Americans who honor the pursuit of liberty. From their stand was born a legend of resistance to tyranny that is still revered, and which transformed the Alamo battlefield into a shrine of honor.

NO QUARTER

Situated on the eastern bank of the San Antonio River, the Alamo was a mission building with a walled compound beside it. A Mexican commander had turned it into a fortified position, but was forced to surrender it to Texan republicans in the fall of 1835. Jim Bowie and James Neill, commanders of the mission, were determined to retain the position. By February 3, 1836, they had received their first

BACKGROUND TO BATTLE

In 1821, the Mexican authorities began encouraging Americans to settle in Texas. By 1830, two U.S. Presidents had offered to buy Texas; these offers put the Mexicans on their guard about control of Texas.

In 1835, General Antonio Lopez de Santa Anna became dictator of Mexico. He prohibited American immigration to Texas and brought Texan affairs under his tight control.

When Texans revolted against Mexican rule in 1835, the U.S. government considered it an internal Mexican affair—it was up to Texans to solve their own problems, aided by volunteers who rallied to their cause.

General Sam Houston, commander of the rebel Texans, realized that there was little he could do against the professional soldiers of Santa Anna's Mexican army and ordered Jim Bowie, commander of the Alamo, to dismantle the Alamo's defenses.

Jim Bowie met fellow Alamo commander, Colonel James Neill, and together they decided to ignore Houston's order and make a stand. Bowie reasoned that a stand here might delay the Mexicans, allowing Houston more time to assemble a bigger army.

Mexican soldiers surge over the Texan defenses on the last day of the Battle of the Alamo. (Painting by H. Charles McBarron.)

reinforcements—30 men, led by William Travis. Five days later came the legendary Davy Crockett and his Tennessee company of mounted volunteers. The strength of the Alamo garrison was 180 combatants and 21 cannons. All were volunteers, and none were professional soldiers. Some were recent immigrants from Britain, including two dozen Englishmen and Irishmen, four Scotsmen, and a Welshman.

The weakest point in the Alamo's defenses was a gap in the perimeter wall between the church and the part of the living quarters known as the low barrack. This was protected by earthworks and four cannons, and Davy Crockett and the Tennesseans pledged to defend it. On the afternoon of February 23, the mission bell sounded, signaling the arrival of Santa Anna's Mexican army. The Mexicans were a seasoned professional force, and came to battle brilliantly uniformed like Napoleonic soldiers. It must have been a daunting sight for the Texans when some 4,000 Mexican troops marched into view, but Travis rejected an offer to surrender. Santa Anna ordered the hoisting of a red flag, signaling that no quarter would be given to the defenders.

The Mexicans began the siege with a bombardment, and gradually moved their artillery closer. But the defenders' rifles proved more accurate than the Mexican muskets, and kept many of the attackers at bay. Travis dispatched several appeals for help, and on March 1, 32 additional volunteers rode through the Mexican lines to enter the Alamo. They were the last to enter—the Mexican artillery was moving closer to the walls. Legend has it that Travis now explained the situation to his men. He drew a line in the dirt with his sword and asked all who wished to remain inside the Alamo to step over it. Every man except one crossed the line; even Jim Bowie, who was sick, and had to be carried across in his bed.

FINAL ASSAULT

At 5:00 A.M. on March 6, the thirteenth day of the siege, Santa Anna launched his final assault on the Alamo. Four columns of Mexican soldiers charged the walls. The Texans responded with a hail of fire from their cannons and rifles, cutting down row after row of Mexicans. Because of their superior numbers, however, the Mexicans were nevertheless able to throw scaling ladders against the walls. The Texans now fought them on the battlements of the mission. Travis was shot through the forehead. The north wall was the first to be breached, and soldiers swarmed into the compound. A fierce firefight followed. Crockett and his Tennesseans were caught in the open, in front of the church, fighting with rifle butts and knives, until they were shot down. Bowie fought from his sickbed, eventually being overwhelmed and bayoneted to death. True to the Mexicans' declaration, no quarter was shown, and all of the Texan defenders were killed. Women, children, and some noncombatants were spared, however, thanks to the intervention of Mexican officers.

The final assault lasted 90 minutes and cost Santa Anna approximately 600 men. Total Mexican losses were 1,544 dead and 500 wounded. The mission was Mexico's, but the heroic stand of its defenders had galvanized support for the Texan cause. Texas proclaimed itself an independent republic on March 2, and on April 21, General Sam Houston—leader of the rebel Texans—and his small Texan army surprised Santa Anna at San Jacinto with howls of "Remember the Alamo!" Santa Anna was captured and forced to recognize the Lone Star Republic. The United States gave its recognition on July 4. The defenders of the Alamo had won the freedom for which they fought. Ironically, that included the "freedom" to own slaves.

Right, *A plan of the Alamo in 1836,* *showing the full extent of the fortified mission.*

THE MEXICAN VIEW

Francis Antonio Ruiz rode with Santa Anna's army, and preserved his account of the fighting on March 6, 1836:

At 3 o'clock pm, General Santa Anna at the head of 4,000 men, advanced against the Alamo. The infantry, artillery and cavalry had formed about 1,000 yards from the walls of the said fortress. The Mexican army charged and were twice repulsed by the deadly fire of Travis' artillery, which resembled a constant thunder. At the third charge the Toluca battalion commenced to scale the walls and suffered severely. Out of 800 men, 130 only were left alive .... The gallantry of the few Texans who defended the Alamo was really wondered at by the Mexican army. Even the generals were astonished at their vigorous resistance, and how dearly victory had been bought.

Quoted in the TEXAS ALMANAC, 1860

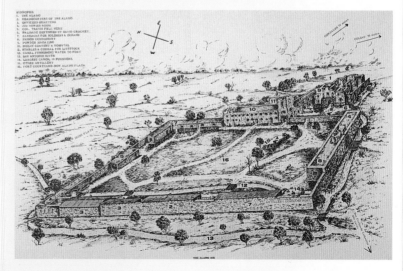

THE ALAMO

Above, *Sam Houston,* *president of the Republic of Texas during its war of independence against Mexico. (Painting by L. Markos.)*

ERECTED IN 1754 as a chapel for Franciscan missionaries, the complex was later used by the Mexican army, and may have become known as the Alamo after its brief occupation by a group of Mexican soldiers whose hometown was Alamo del Parras. In 1849, the U.S. army repaired the mission buildings and replaced the upper portion of the now famous facade.

In 1876, a building was erected on top of the walls of the long barrack, and this became a store. In 1903, it was offered for sale as a hotel, but it was bought instead by Clara Driscoll, a Daughter of the Republic of Texas—a society devoted to the memory of the struggle for Texan independence. Two years later, the State purchased it from her, and turned it into a shrine to be maintained by the Daughters of the Republic of Texas.

One of the few survivors of the Alamo was Mrs. Dickinson, who escaped the slaughter with her child and 14 other noncombatants. "The struggle lasted more than two hours," she recalled. Three unarmed gunners, who had to abandon their cannon, were shot down at Mrs. Dickinson's side. One of them spoke to her about his wife and four children. When the Mexicans finally burst in, they bayoneted him, threw him in the air like a bundle of straw, and then shot him.

A Mexican officer then entered the church and spoke to her in English: "Are you Mrs. Dickinson?" She nodded, and he said, "If you wish to save your life, follow me." She obeyed, and although she was shot and wounded, her life and her child were spared. As she walked across the courtyard in front of the church, she saw heaps of the dead and dying. "182 Texans and 1,600 Mexicans were killed," she recorded. She recognized Davy Crockett, lying dead and mutilated between the church and the two-story barracks. "Col. Bowie was sick in bed and not expected to live," she remembered, "but as the vicious Mexicans entered his room, he killed two of them with his pistols before they pierced him through with their sabers .... Col. Travis and Bonham were killed while working the cannon, the body of the former lay on top of the church."

PLAN OF BATTLE

The Alamo position comprised a church and a walled compound—an area of approximately three acres (1,200 square meters), defended by 12-foot (365-centimeter) high walls. Long buildings, known as barracks, ran along the inside of the walls; they were used as living quarters by the Texans. The fighting defenders numbered about 180 men, with 21 cannons. The attacking Mexican army numbered 4,000 men.

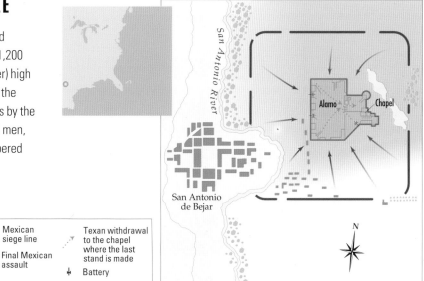

San Antonio River

Alamo Chapel

San Antonio de Bejar

| — | Mexican siege line |
| ↗ | Final Mexican assault |
| Texan withdrawal to the chapel where the last stand is made |
| ↓ | Battery |

N

THE ALAMO

S AN ANTONIO—the home of the Alamo—is the most charming city in Texas, bisected by a beautiful river fringed with lush tropical plants. The Alamo lies at the heart of downtown San Antonio, and is a favorite tourist location. Today it is an icon of American liberty, but for many years the ruins were ignored.

GETTING THERE

LOCATION:

300 Alamao Plaza, San Antonio, Texas.

VISITOR INFORMATION:

Daughters of the Republic of Texas, P.O. Box 2599, San Antonio, TX 78299.

TELEPHONE:

210-225-1391

DIRECTIONS: *Interstate highways to San Antonio; I-10 from Houston, and I-35 from Austin and Dallas. The Alamo is in San Antonio's central downtown area.*

TOUR DISTANCE:

1¾ miles (3 km).

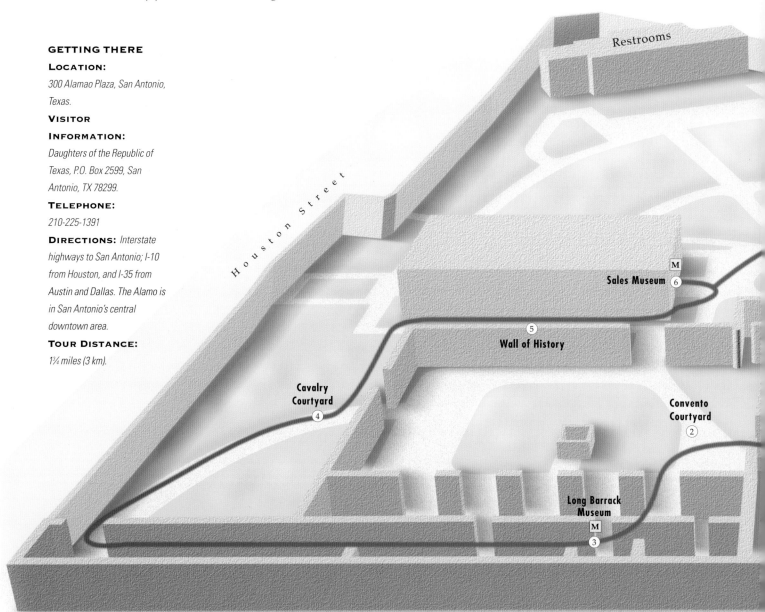

Restrooms

Houston Street

Sales Museum M 6

Wall of History 5

Cavalry Courtyard 4

Convento Courtyard 2

Long Barrack Museum M 3

Alamo Plaza

Right, *The long barrack (2), now without a roof.* *The second floor of this two-story building was used as a hospital during the siege, and the first floor housed an armory and living quarters. The barrack was the scene of the last stand by second-in-command Captain John Baugh and other Texans on the final day of the battle.*

ALAMO CHURCH

*The church was built in 1758, but remained unfinished in 1836. Its
northwest corner was used as a powder magazine during the siege.
Irishman Major Robert Evans tried to ignite it at the end of the battle,
but he was shot down.*

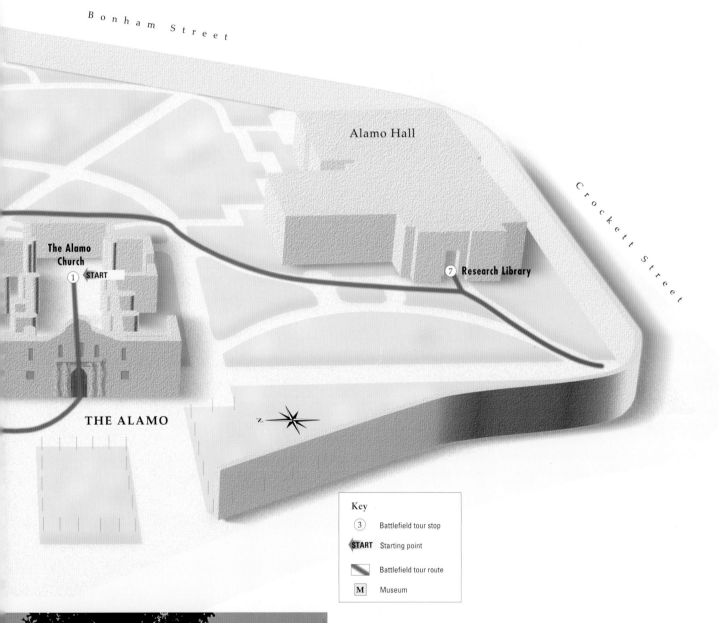

Bonham Street

Alamo Hall

Crockett Street

The Alamo
Church
① START

⑦ Research Library

THE ALAMO

Key

③   Battlefield tour stop

START   Starting point

   Battlefield tour route

M   Museum

Left, *The Alamo today, in downtown San Antonio.* *The
facade (1) has been restored. In 1836, however, the round
gable over the doorway had already been destroyed.*

BLOODY DAY

Above, ***Confederate General Robert E. Lee*** *with his fellow commander Major General T. J. "Stonewall" Jackson.*

Left, ***View from the west end of Bloody Lane.*** *Wooden palisades were used to transform the sunken road into a formidable part of the Confederate line.*

IN WESTERN MARYLAND, beside a stream called Antietam Creek, two armies collided on the single bloodiest day of the Civil War. On a hot September day, more than 23,000 American soldiers fell—over seven times the U.S. losses on the bloody beaches of Tarawa in the Pacific in World War II. The Battle of Antietam cruelly demonstrated the gap between tactics and weapons at this time. Generals still hoped to win battles with sweeping Napoleonic strategy, but their men were brought down by the ferocity of improved firepower.

TO SHARPSBURG

Confederate General Robert E. Lee was leading an aggressive campaign to invade the North when he established his headquarters in the town of Sharpsburg beside the Potomac River. Union Major General George B. McClellan had followed Lee's movements over the previous days. When he saw that the Confederates were caught between the Potomac, at their rear, and Antietam Creek, McClellan prepared to attack. He assembled his 87,000-strong army on the eastern side of the creek. Lee knew that his position was not ideal. With only 41,000 men to confront the enemy, he ordered the creation of strong defensive positions along his

BACKGROUND TO BATTLE

The agricultural South knew that it could not win a war of attrition with the industrial North. But it had won several battles, and Confederate President Davis approved General Robert E. Lee's plan to invade the North, in the hope that it might encourage Britain and France to recognize the Confederacy and provide assistance.

At the beginning of September 1862, Lee crossed the Potomac River near Leesburg with some 41,000 men. He moved northward into Pennsylvania with the cavalry troops of Major General J. E. B. Stuart acting as a screen.

Meanwhile, Union Major General George B. McClellan gathered an army of 87,000 men in Washington, and tracked Lee's movements.

From September 12 to 14 Lee's army was spread out and vulnerable, but McClellan failed to take advantage of this, allowing Lee's army to reassemble at Sharpsburg.

Confederate Major General T. J. "Stonewall" Jackson captured Harpers Ferry on September 15 before joining Lee. McClellan again failed to attack before Lee received these reinforcements and began preparing his positions at Sharpsburg.

line. His rapid understanding of the defensive possibilities of the landscape proved decisive in the ensuing conflict.

McClellan began the Union assault at 6:00 A.M. with an attack on the extreme left flank of the Confederate army in the cornfield around the Dunker Church in the northern part of the battlefield. Confederate soldiers hid among the tall stalks of corn and surprised the advancing Union soldiers with a tremendous hail of fire. Union artillery responded by blasting the corn until the field was a devastated mass of scythed corn and bodies. Confederates fled the slaughter, many falling at Hagerstown Pike as Union soldiers charged forward, sensing victory. Confederate soldiers made a stand at the Dunker Church, and the fighting halted around

Above, *Dead artillery crew* on the left flank of the Confederate position at Antietam, with the Dunker Church in the background.

President Abraham Lincoln later visited the battlefield of Antietam on October 4, 1862 to meet the Union generals who had bravely participated in the terrible battle. (Photograph by Mathew Brady.)

this position. Major General T. J. "Stonewall" Jackson, commander of the Confederate left flank, hid reinforcements in the West Woods, and when overconfident Union forces failed to spot them, closed the trap, striking down more than 2,000 men in 20 minutes.

Having so nearly broken the Confederate line, only to fail, McClellan switched the thrust of his assault farther south, to the center of Lee's position. At 10:30 A.M., lines of Union soldiers marched toward the sunken road, a ditch behind a wooden fence that Lee had turned into a fortified trench. For over three hours, Confederate soldiers fired relentlessly into the advancing troops. The blue lines faltered, attacked, fell back, attacked again. Neither side lacked courage. Lee sent in his last reserves to hold the road, but a mistaken order caused some of the Confederates to fall back. The sudden gap allowed Union soldiers to rake the position with fire. The sunken road was transformed into a bloody lane, with bodies heaped along the ditch. By 1:00 P.M., both sides were exhausted and the fighting halted. If McClellan had sent in his reserves at this point he would have won the battle. Instead, a fatal caution stayed his hand. Meanwhile, a new attack had begun farther south on the battlefield.

General McClellan, commander of the Union army at Antietam. His caution in committing soldiers to the battle threw away opportunities to win the day.

BURNSIDE'S BRIDGE

Major General Ambrose E. Burnside led the Union left wing across the Rohrbach bridge over Antietam Creek. His troops could easily have marched through the shallow water, but,

because of a lack of reconnaissance, he funneled his men across the stone bridge, directly into Confederate fire. At 1:00 P.M. Union forces launched a more concerted attack, took the bridge, and marched toward Sharpsburg. It seemed that Lee's luck had finally run out—but at 4:00 P.M., Major General Ambrose Powell Hill arrived from across the Potomac with a division of veteran Confederate soldiers. They plowed into Burnside's troops, creating confusion among the men, who believed they had won the battle. Union lines broke and fell back to the creek. The day's fighting was over. Neither side had won, neither side had lost.

Both sides were exhausted. The next day, Lee considered a counteroffensive, but his men were too weak, and the following night the Confederate army withdrew across the Potomac. Lee had defeated an army twice the size of his own. But both sides had sustained devastating casualties, and Lee's drive to take the war to the North had been stopped.

A NEAR MISS

The day before the Battle of Antietam, the two sides assembled on either side of the creek. Bob Patterson, a Union soldier in the 19th Indiana Volunteers of the Iron Brigade, who crossed the creek with his comrades and came under fire, almost became the victim of a bizarre accident:

In passing where the enemy had killed some cattle, some of our boys had detached strips of fat from the intestines of the animals which they applied to their guns to prevent rust. I had unconsciously raised the hammer of my gun and was applying the grease about the tube as the regiment halted, when I rested the muzzle of the gun against my left shoulder, and in drawing the string of fat through the guard the gun was discharged, and the ball passing through the rim of my hat.

Quoted in ON MANY A BLOODY FIELD *by Alan D. Gaff (Indiana University Press, 1996).*

Union troops surge over Burnside's Bridge near the end of the Battle of Antietam. (Lithograph by Kurz & Allison.)

ANTIETAM

Major General D. H. Hill

commanded the Confederate troops that hung on grimly to their position in the sunken road.

THE ANTIETAM NATIONAL BATTLEFIELD was established in 1890 to commemorate the sacrifices made by both Union and Confederate troops there, and to preserve the main features of the battlefield. Today, the scene of the bloody conflict is framed by rolling hills and picturesque farmland. Antietam Creek is fringed by lush greenery. It is difficult to associate this spot with the horror that so many men faced there in September 1862.

The sunken road is partly recreated, with the wooden obstacles that turned it into a fortified trench. To the south of the Dunker Church, the road running between Hagerstown Pike—today marked by a wooden fence—and Boonsborough Turnpike saw some of the day's fiercest fighting, which earned it the name "Bloody Lane." Five Confederate brigades were posted here, under the command of Major General D. H. Hill. Drawn at first into the fighting around the Dunker Church, they were forced back to the road, where they piled up fenceposts as hasty defenses. Divisions of Union troops advanced toward them in steady lines despite being bombarded by musket and rifle fire. The Union troops gave way, but another division joined them. Confederate commander Lee could see that the sunken road had become a crucial point of the battle. He ordered his own reserves forward to hold the position.

In this small area, control of the battle swayed between the Confederate and Union troops with only one result—mass slaughter on both sides. One soldier said that there were so many dead on the road that you could walk down it without touching the ground. As the fighting receded at the sunken road, another stage of the battle was only just beginning to the south around Rohrbach bridge, now known as Burnside's Bridge after the Union commander who eventually took the bridge at the cost of great loss of life to those under his command.

PLAN OF BATTLE

This map shows the main thrusts and counterthrusts of the Battle of Antietam. The Union attack began in the north of the battlefield with an advance through the cornfield to the Dunker Church. The battle then moved southward to the sunken road. The third phase occurred in the south, where Burnside broke through the lower bridge, only to be hurled back by A. P. Hill's late—yet timely—arrival. Lee fielded about 41,000 men against McClellan's 87,000 (including reserves), although some 20,000 of these Union soldiers were kept in reserve. At the end of the battle, Lee had suffered 10,700 casualties, and McClellan 12,410.

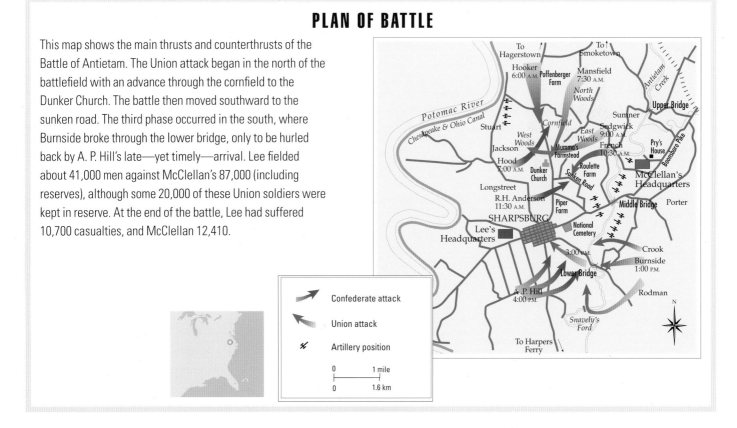

ANTIETAM

ANTIETAM IS NOTORIOUS for being the single bloodiest day of the American Civil War—over 23,000 men were killed and wounded. The ghosts of this sacrifice give the battlefield a brooding atmosphere. Now a perfectly preserved National Park, the sunken road, or "Bloody Lane,"—the defensive position the Confederates held while countless lines of Union soldiers advanced into the withering fire—dominates its center.

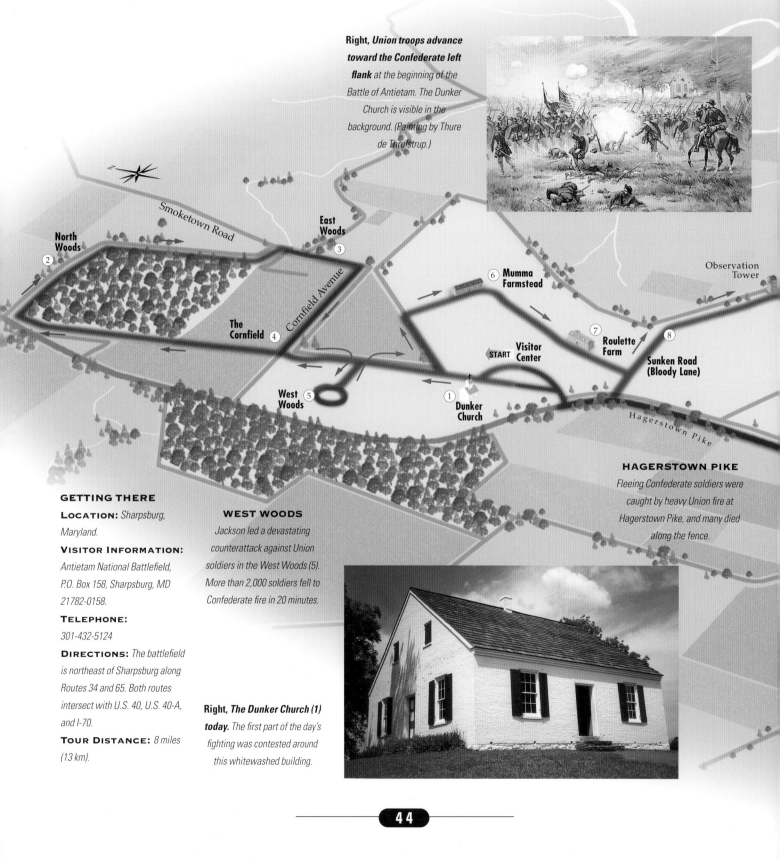

Right, *Union troops advance toward the Confederate left flank* at the beginning of the Battle of Antietam. The Dunker Church is visible in the background. (Painting by Thure de Thrulstrup.)

Observation Tower

North Woods

Smoketown Road

East Woods

3

The Cornfield 4

Cornfield Avenue

6 Mumma Farmstead

7

Roulette Farm

8

Sunken Road (Bloody Lane)

START Visitor Center

West Woods 5

1 Dunker Church

2

Hagerstown Pike

HAGERSTOWN PIKE

Fleeing Confederate soldiers were caught by heavy Union fire at Hagerstown Pike, and many died along the fence.

GETTING THERE

LOCATION: *Sharpsburg, Maryland.*

VISITOR INFORMATION: *Antietam National Battlefield, P.O. Box 158, Sharpsburg, MD 21782-0158.*

TELEPHONE: *301-432-5124*

DIRECTIONS: *The battlefield is northeast of Sharpsburg along Routes 34 and 65. Both routes intersect with U.S. 40, U.S. 40-A, and I-70.*

TOUR DISTANCE: *8 miles (13 km).*

WEST WOODS

Jackson led a devastating counterattack against Union soldiers in the West Woods (5). More than 2,000 soldiers fell to Confederate fire in 20 minutes.

Right, *The Dunker Church (1) today.* *The first part of the day's fighting was contested around this whitewashed building.*

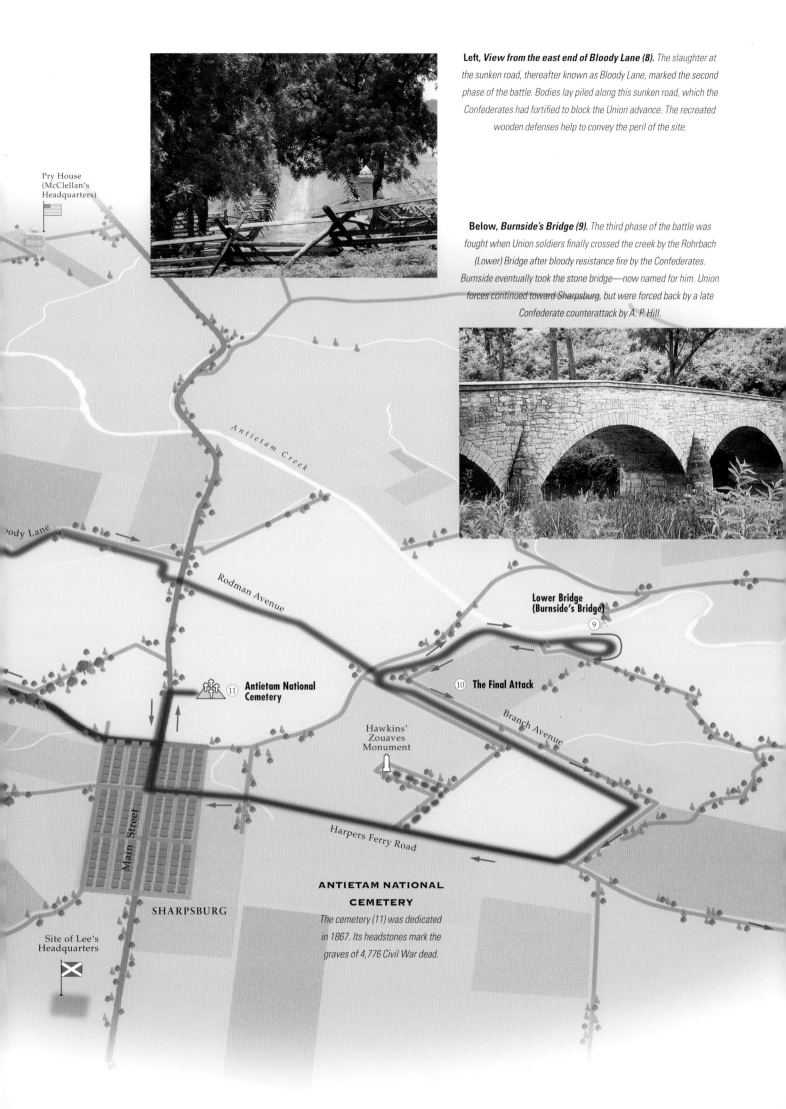

Left, *View from the east end of Bloody Lane (8).* *The slaughter at the sunken road, thereafter known as Bloody Lane, marked the second phase of the battle. Bodies lay piled along this sunken road, which the Confederates had fortified to block the Union advance. The recreated wooden defenses help to convey the peril of the site.*

Below, *Burnside's Bridge (9).* *The third phase of the battle was fought when Union soldiers finally crossed the creek by the Rohrbach (Lower) Bridge after bloody resistance fire by the Confederates. Burnside eventually took the stone bridge—now named for him. Union forces continued toward Sharpsburg, but were forced back by a late Confederate counterattack by A. P. Hill.*

Pry House (McClellan's Headquarters)

Antietam Creek

Bloody Lane

Rodman Avenue

Lower Bridge (Burnside's Bridge)
⑨

⑩ The Final Attack

Branch Avenue

✝ ⑪ Antietam National Cemetery

Hawkins' Zouaves Monument

Main Street

SHARPSBURG

Harpers Ferry Road

ANTIETAM NATIONAL CEMETERY
The cemetery (11) was dedicated in 1867. Its headstones mark the graves of 4,776 Civil War dead.

Site of Lee's Headquarters

BATTLE FOR THE WEST

Above, *The Battle of Shiloh,* showing Union soldiers resisting Confederate assaults. Trees blasted by artillery became a feature of the battlefield.

Left, *The Tennessee River* was well used by the Union army during the Battle of Shiloh. Not only did the river provide access for reinforcements, but fire from river gunboats stopped Confederate advances from reaching Pittsburg Landing.

BACKGROUND TO BATTLE

The North's grand strategy was to command the Mississippi River, advance south, and split the Confederacy in two.

Union Major General Ulysses S. Grant began this objective in early 1862 with an amphibious assault along the Tennessee River, using a squadron of ironclad river gunboats.

Union forces captured Fort Henry on February 6, and Fort Donelson surrendered on February 16. Grant seized Nashville on February 25.

Grant's planned advance on Corinth, a strategically important railroad junction, was halted when he was ordered to wait for Major General Don Carlos Buell to catch up with him on the Tennessee River.

It was then that Confederate General Albert Sidney Johnston, based in Corinth, decided to take the battle to the Union troops, and pounced on Grant near Shiloh Church.

BOTH NORTH AND SOUTH entered the Battle of Shiloh with illusions of easy success. The inexperienced volunteer armies still believed that the war could be quickly won. After Shiloh, both sides knew it would be a long campaign. Modern firepower impacted hugely on the enthusiastic formations—more than one-fifth of the combined forces became casualties.

HORNET'S NEST

In mid-March, Union Major General Ulysses S. Grant was ordered to wait on the Tennessee River for reinforcements led by Major General Don Carlos Buell. Confederate General Albert Sidney Johnston was determined to attack before these arrived. Fighting broke out early on the morning of April 6, when scouting skirmishers from both sides collided. Union Brigadier General William T. Sherman reinforced his position near Shiloh Church, but the Confederates launched an all-out attack. The Union line faltered, as many of its newly recruited soldiers fled from their first experience under fire. Elsewhere, Union troops rallied in a densely wooded area along an old sunken road. It became known as the Hornet's Nest, because of the stinging fire inflicted on the attacking Confederates.

General Grant heard the cannon fire at Shiloh, and sailed up the Tennessee River in a steamer. He ordered Buell to advance his men to a point on the riverbank opposite the battlefield. Grant reorganized the Union defense along the ridge at Shiloh Church. Relentless Confederate attacks pushed the Union line back. General Johnston personally led a charge to maintain the momentum, but a Union bullet severed the artery in his leg, and he died from loss of blood at 2:30 P.M. His sudden death caused a lull in the fighting, until General P. G. T. Beauregard, his second-in-command, took over.

Beauregard concentrated the Confederate attack on the Hornet's Nest, ordering 62 cannons to open fire on the Union forces. Union soldiers to the left and the right of the position retreated, but the center (commanded by Major General W. H. L. Wallace and Brigadier General Benjamin Prentiss) held firm, although increasingly isolated. Fearing encirclement, Wallace finally gave the order to fall back, under heavy

Right, *The Union counterattack* during the Battle of Shiloh, with the Tennessee River in the background. (Contemporary lithograph by Kurz and Allison.)

crossfire, through a ravine that became known as Hell's Hollow. Prentiss maintained resistance until late in the afternoon, but eventually surrendered more than 2,000 men.

SECOND DAY

Night brought a break in the fighting, but not in Grant's resolve to improve his position. Buell ferried some 17,000 troops across the river to reinforce Grant, and Union gunboats *Lexington* and *Tyler* kept the Confederates awake by bombarding them every 15 minutes. The Confederates—who possessed the battlefield apart from the Pittsburg Landing next to the river—were convinced that they had won the

GENERAL UNDER FIRE

Major General Ulysses S. Grant, later President of the United States, wrote his own account of the Battle of Shiloh, at which he commanded the Union forces. On the second day of the battle, he came under fire himself:

There did not appear to be an enemy to our right, until suddenly a battery with musketry opened upon us from the edge of the woods on the other side of clearing. The shells and balls whistled about our ears very fast for about a minute. I do not think it took us longer than that to get out of range and out of sight. In the sudden start we made, Major Hawkins lost his hat. He did not stop to pick it up. When we arrived at a perfectly safe position we halted to take an account of damages. McPherson's horse was panting as if ready to drop. On examination it was found that a ball had struck him forward of the flank just back of the saddle, and had gone entirely through. In a few minutes the poor beast dropped dead; he had given no sign of injury until we came to a stop. A ball had struck the metal scabbard of my sword, just below the hilt, and broken it nearly off; before the battle was over it had broken off entirely.

From PERSONAL MEMOIRS OF U. S. GRANT
(New York, 1885).

General U. S. Grant, commander of the Union forces at the Battle of Shiloh.

¡Right, *Edwin Tennison,* a young volunteer in the Confederate army from Georgia, who was killed in action in July 1862. For the many raw recruits involved, Shiloh was the first experience of coming under fire in a major battle.

Right, *New York State Militiaman* *with percussion rifle-musket, the most popular weapon in the Civil War. The rifled barrel caused the bullet to spin when leaving the musket, increasing accuracy and range.*

battle. At daybreak, the Union army took the initiative and attacked. The Confederates were disorganized, and retreated across the territory they had gained, including the Hornet's Nest. Union Major General Lew Wallace's 3rd Division wreaked vengeance for the previous day by throwing the Confederates back toward Shiloh Church. Elsewhere, charge followed countercharge, as neither side was willing to give way. Confusion ruled, and many Confederates fired on their own troops, misled by the multiplicity of uniform colors.

Beauregard pinned his hopes on Confederate reinforcements from Corinth, but the Union army was equally determined to deny him and pressed on. By 2:00 P.M., Beauregard recognized that it was useless to continue, and organized an orderly retreat toward Corinth. Grant did not pursue him, realizing that his men were too exhausted. Heavy rain turned the roads to mud. Union cavalry urged pursuit, but a skirmish with a screening force of Rebel cavalry, led by Colonel Nathan Bedford Forrest, at Fallen Timbers discouraged them.

It was a costly conflict. Neither side lacked courage, but frontal charges into musket, rifle, and artillery fire were deadly. Out of 65,085 Union troops, 1,754 were killed, 8,408 wounded, and 2,885 missing. Of the 44,699 Confederates, 1,728 were killed, 8,012 wounded, and 959 missing. Both sides claimed victory. Strategically, the North had gained the advantage; the Confederates were compelled to retreat southward, and the Union would win the "Battle of the West."

SHILOH

One of the most intense points of the Battle of Shiloh was at the Hornet's Nest. Parts of three Union divisions huddled behind the trench provided by a sunken road in a peach orchard. Confederate troops attacked the position 11 times. Confederate General Johnston was in the midst of the action, and personally led several attacks on horseback. He waved a little tin cup at his troops, a trophy seized as he rode through a Union camp. This was the act of a medieval-style commander, personally inspiring his troops, using his fearless character to urge them forward as he dug his spurs into his horse.

Just before noon on the first day of battle, General Johnston prepared his men for another attack on the left flank of the Hornet's Nest. "A few more charges and the day is ours!" he shouted to soldiers of the 9th Arkansas Brigade. They were a passionate group of volunteers, who brought with them some of their personal weapons, including hunting rifles, double-barreled shotguns, and large-bladed bowie knives. Johnston knew this and played on it in his words to them: "They say you boast of your prowess with the bowie knife. Today you wield a nobler weapon, the bayonet. Employ it well." Johnston wanted to take the Union position at the point of the bayonet. It was a do-or-die approach, in which he hoped that the sight of lines of soldiers wielding bayonets would make the Union soldiers turn and run.

Just before 2:00 P.M., Johnston personally led three Confederate brigades toward the Union position in the Peach Orchard. Bullets whined past him, inflicting casualties on the troops he led forward. A bullet tore off the toe of one of his boots, but did not harm him, and he rode on. A second bullet caused more damage, although at first he did not realize it and made light of his injury. The bullet passed through the calf of his right leg, but severed an artery, and the blood drained into his boot. Within a half-hour of leading his troops into battle, the general was dead, and the battle turned against the Confederate army.

PLAN OF BATTLE

The Confederate army took the initiative at Shiloh and pressed forward in a series of frontal attacks that caused the Union army to fall back from Shiloh Church toward Pittsburg Landing. During the night of the first day, the Union army was reinforced with troops ferried across to the Landing. Next day, the Union army counterattacked and won back the land that it had lost.

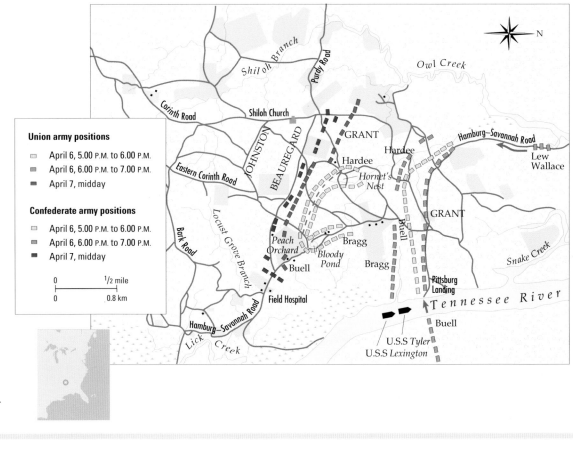

Union army positions
- April 6, 5.00 P.M. to 6.00 P.M.
- April 6, 6.00 P.M. to 7.00 P.M.
- April 7, midday

Confederate army positions
- April 6, 5.00 P.M. to 6.00 P.M.
- April 6, 6.00 P.M. to 7.00 P.M.
- April 7, midday

0 — 1/2 mile
0 — 0.8 km

SHILOH

THE TENNESSEE RIVER flows past Shiloh National Military Park, reminding the battlefield tourist of its importance in the two-day conflict. Without reinforcements ferried across the water to Pittsburg Landing, Grant would have faced defeat. The landscape is heavily wooded, and walking beneath the trees today is highly pleasurable—in stark contrast to the scene of 1862, when boughs were shredded and trunks splintered by artillery and musket fire.

Hardee Road

Beauregard Road

Shiloh Branch

Peabody Road

Federal Road

Gladen Road

Hornet's Nest Road

Sunken Road

Confederate Drive

SHILOH CHURCH

A new church stands on the site of the original Shiloh Church (6), on the ridge where the Union army made its first stand against the Confederates.

(6) **Shiloh Church**

Confederate Burial Trench

(4)

(5) **Illinois State Monument**

(7) **Hornet's Nest and Sunken Road**

(10) **Bloody Pond**

Johnsto...

Peach Orchard

(9)

(8) **Johnston's Monument**

PEACH ORCHARD

Hard fighting took place in the Peach Orchard (9) where the trees were in full bloom. The blossoms fell to cover the dead.

BLOODY POND

The Union army retreated past a shallow pond (10), where the injured of both sides tended their wounds, turning the water red.

GETTING THERE

LOCATION: *West bank of the Tennessee River, near Corinth.*

VISITOR INFORMATION: *Shiloh National Military Park, 1055 Pittsburg Landing, Shiloh, TN 38376.*

TELEPHONE: *901-689-5696*

DIRECTIONS: *Shiloh is off Route 22, 25 miles (40 km) northeast of Corinth and 110 miles (177 km) east of Tennessee.*

TOUR DISTANCE: *9½ miles (15.5 km).*

Key

(3) Battlefield tour stop

START Starting point

▨ Battlefield tour route

⌷ Monument

✝ Church

CONFEDERATE MONUMENT

The Confederate Monument (3) was raised in 1917 to commemorate the Southern troops who died at the battle. In the center is a bust of General Albert S. Johnston, who was killed on the first day of battle.

Above, Captain Hickenlooper's Battery in the Hornet's Nest. *The Hornet's Nest (7), was a wooded area around a sunken road. It earned its name from the stinging shots launched by Union soldiers as they fought to repel 11 Confederate attacks on this position. The fire from 62 Confederate cannons finally forced the Northerners to fall back.*

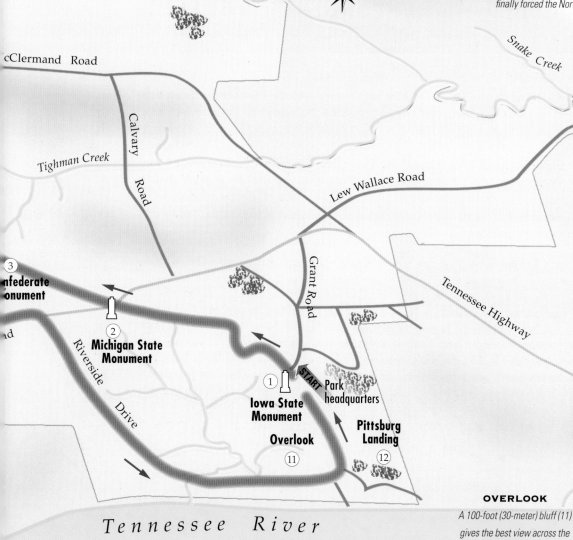

IOWA STATE MONUMENT

The 75-foot (23-meter) Iowa State Monument (1), surmounted by a bronze eagle, was erected in 1906. Surviving cannons nearby mark the Union line at the close of the first day of battle.

PITTSBURG LANDING

The Union army held its position at Pittsburg Landing (12), enabling reinforcements to be ferried across the river during the night. Its counterattack was launched from here the next day. A Visitor Center is located near the site.

OVERLOOK

A 100-foot (30-meter) bluff (11) gives the best view across the Tennessee River to the point where Buell embarked his army.

Lincoln's Gettysburg Address

November 19, 1863

Four score and seven years ago our fathers brought forth on this continent, a new nation, conceived in liberty, and dedicated to the proposition that all men are created equal.

Now we are engaged in a great civil war, testing whether that nation, or any nation so conceived and so dedicated, can long endure. We are met on a great battlefield of that war. We have come to dedicate a portion of that field, as a final resting place for those who here gave their lives that that nation might live. It is altogether fitting and proper that we should do this.

But, in a larger sense, we can not dedicate ~ we can not consecrate ~ we can not hallow ~ this ground. The brave men, living and dead, who struggled here have consecrated it, far above our poor power to add or detract. The world will little note, nor long remember what we say here, but it can never forget what they did here. It is for us the living, rather, to be dedicated here to the unfinished work which they who fought here have thus far so nobly advanced. It is rather for us to be here dedicated to the great task remaining before us ~ that from these honored dead we take increased devotion to that cause for which they gave the last full measure of devotion ~ that we here highly resolve that these dead shall not have died in vain ~ that this nation, under God, shall have a new birth of freedom ~ and that government of the people, by the people, for the people, shall not perish from the earth.

BIRTH OF FREEDOM

Above, **General Robert E. Lee,** the charismatic commander of the Confederate army at Gettysburg.

Left, *A contemporary print of Abraham Lincoln's Gettysburg Address.* The President delivered his famous address on the site of what is now the National Cemetery, the burial ground for many who sacrificed their lives on the battlefield.

ORE MEN FOUGHT AND DIED during the Battle of Gettysburg than in any other battle fought on North American soil. It was one of the last heroic blows struck by the Confederacy, and marked a turning point in the Civil War. Four months after the conflict, President Abraham Lincoln visited the battlefield and gave his famous Gettysburg Address, in which he spoke of the "new birth of freedom" brought about by this terrible sacrifice, and declared that "government of the people, by the people, for the people, shall not perish from the earth."

LEE'S LAST STAND

The Battle of Gettysburg began by accident. General Robert E. Lee was pursuing an aggressive campaign and threatening the northern capital of Washington. He concentrated his men at Cashtown, Pennsylvania, operating without definite knowledge of an approaching Union army. Reconnaissance was usually provided by Lee's cavalry, but a raid had diverted two of his three cavalry brigades. On June 30, a brigade of

BACKGROUND TO BATTLE

The events of June 1863 mirrored those of the previous year that had culminated at Antietam. The Confederate leaders knew that they could not afford a drawn-out war, and they sought to shock the North into negotiation by invading their territory.

Confederate General Robert E. Lee had achieved a victory at Chancellorsville in early May, and hoped to maintain his momentum. He pushed on into the Shenandoah Valley, his movements once again screened by Major General J. E. B. Stuart.

Another Confederate victory followed when Major General Richard S. Ewell won the second battle of Winchester on June 14. Morale was high as Lee crossed the Potomac with 76,000 men.

Union Major General Joseph Hooker shadowed Lee's movements, but, like Major General George B. McClellan before him, failed to strike when the Confederate army was stretched out. Hooker resigned and was replaced by Major General George Meade.

Stuart left to raid the rear of the Union Army in central Maryland, while Lee concentrated his troops at Cashtown. There, events overtook Lee and dragged him into battle.

Confederate soldiers approached Gettysburg as the vanguard of a "reconnaissance force" ordered by Lee to occupy the town. There, they collided with a scouting party of Union soldiers. Each side fired on the other, and the Confederates forced the Union troops back. Word of the conflict spread, and increasing numbers of troops joined the fighting.

On July 1, the Confederates initially gained the upper hand. Lee thought it wise to exploit the situation, hoping to catch the Union forces off balance. He moved his entire army to the town of Gettysburg. Realizing that they had to hold their position until the rest of their army arrived, the Union soldiers took command of a long spur of high ground that overlooked the town. This decision determined the shape of the battle to come.

On the morning of July 2, 1863, Major General George Meade and his Northern army occupied the high ground running from Culp's Hill on their right flank, along Cemetery Ridge in the center, to Little Round Top on the left. Lee had now lost the advantage of surprise, and was forced to mirror the Union formation by deploying his troops below the high ground. He then lost more time waiting for reinforcements. Meanwhile, additional Northern troops joined Meade. Lee finally decided to attack in the late afternoon. A mighty artillery bombardment began the assault, and Major General Richard S. Ewell, commander of Lee's II Corps, launched a diversionary attack at Culp's Hill. Lee's main target was Little Round Top, where he hoped Lieutenant General James Longstreet's I Corps would crush the weak Union left flank and turn

Confederate participants reenact scenes *from the battle on the site of the fighting at Gettysburg.*

in on the center. Meade was dealing with Ewell's diversionary attack, and could not spare men for Little Round Top.

Confederates surged up the wooded slopes toward Little Round Top. At the extreme end of the Union left flank stood the 20th Maine, commanded by Colonel Joshua L. Chamberlain, a college professor who believed passionately in the Northern cause. He would not give up his position. Line after line of Alabama troops hurled themselves at the men from Maine. The combatants were shrouded in fire and smoke, and neither side would yield. Ferocious hand-to-hand fighting broke out. Chamberlain could see that his line was thinning, and decided on a do-or-die order. "Bayonet!" he shouted. The men of Maine roared their approval, then charged downhill at the Confederates. The effect was overwhelming, and the gray-clad troops gave way. Lee had fared better elsewhere, but Meade would not be shifted. The day ended without a victory for either side.

PICKETT'S CHARGE

The next day, both sides received reinforcements. Having failed to turn either flank, Lee decided to make a Napoleonic thrust into the middle of Meade's army, using some 15,000 Confederate troops to split it in two. Major General George E. Pickett was only one of three divisional commanders leading the troops, but his name would forever be associated with the attack—perhaps to protect the reputation of a revered superior. The assault began at 1:00 P.M. with a two-hour artillery bombardment of Cemetery Ridge. Meade sensed the threat of a major attack on his center, and reinforced it with troops from his flanks. By mid-afternoon, the Confederates had begun their advance through the wheatfields toward the Northern center.

As the Confederates drew closer, Union artillery opened up, slicing through the lines of gray. The Southerners pushed on, to be met by a heavy volley of musket fire; the lines shuddered as men fell beneath the hail of lead. Meade then ordered a previously hidden force of artillery to open up with a devastating crossfire. Confederate Brigadier General Lewis A. Armistead thrust his sword into his hat and held it high. "Come on boys!" he shouted, "Give them the cold steel! Who will follow me?" Of the 15,000 men who began the assault, only Armistead and 150 men reached the stone wall defending the Union position. Armistead placed his hand on an abandoned Union cannon and was immediately cut down by Northern bullets. This moment of supreme bravery, and the location where it took place, has been called the "high water mark" of the Confederacy. But, it was not nearly enough. Meade annihilated the breakthrough with a counterattack. For Lee it was all over, and he withdrew his men before Meade could pursue him. Union casualties for the three days were 3,155 killed, 14,529 wounded, and 5,365 missing. Confederate casualties were 3,903 killed, 18,735 wounded, and 5,425 missing.

FACING PICKETT'S CHARGE

Steven Allen Osborn was a soldier in Major General Winfield Scott Hancock's II Corps of the Army of the Potomac. At the Battle of Gettysburg, he faced the Confederate advance known as Pickett's Charge:

Now the enemy's guns have quieted down and our heads are poking up above the breastwork all along the line. Then the cry is raised "There they come!" It was a grand, but awful sight to see those three lines sweeping forward to almost certain death. First there is the report of one lone cannon up to our right, quickly followed by the most awful, unearthly roar of the letting go of some 60 guns along our line. To the right of us their line kept advancing but opposite us we could see they were staggered and were giving ground but rallied and came on. The gunners had loaded as directed and as soon as they could see the effect of their guns through the smoke they quickly lowered the muzzles of their guns and the cans slid out. The guns were reloaded as at first, and the enemy received another raking fire. That settled the matter as far as those of us were concerned but not so on our right, they came up to and even over our breastwork. It was no use however, those that were not killed were taken prisoner and Pickett's charge had utterly failed.

Quoted in SHENANGO VALLEY NEWS *(Greenville, Pennsylvania, 1915).*

A reenactment of Pickett's Charge *near the battlefield at Gettysburg.*

GETTYSBURG

"Sharpshooter's Last Sleep": this photograph was taken by Mathew Brady shortly after the fighting ended at Little Round Top.

GETTYSBURG, PENNSYLVANIA IS a quiet town, but for three days in 1863 it was the focal point of the Civil War.

The area known as Cemetery Hill assumed its importance on the first day of the battle, when Union troops retreated to the high ground nearby. The Confederates' failure to take this position immediately was a major error, because it was reinforced throughout the night. The Union position was formidable and Lee's subordinates suggested caution, but Lee wanted a dashing victory.

The fighting on the second day was anchored toward the south of the battlefield, against the Union left flank. Confederate troops surged through Devil's Den and ascended Little Round Top. A bulge in the Union lines—"Sickles' salient"— was crushed, and at Trostle farm a Union gun battery was captured. Full of optimism, the Confederates advanced northward toward the center of the Union line, held by the 1st Minnesota Infantry, along Cemetery Ridge.

Fearlessly, the Minnesotans charged the Confederates, sacrificing themselves to give the Union army time to reinforce the line. With the heroic Union defense of Little Top farther south, the Confederate attack ground to a halt. Lee had failed to achieve his dashing success.

PLAN OF BATTLE

The Battle of Gettysburg was fought over three days. Confederate forces first concentrated on the town. Union forces then retreated to the high ground leading from Culp's Hill, along Cemetery Ridge to Little Round Top. On the second day, Lee attacked the right and left flanks of the Union position. On the third day, he assaulted the center of the Union position.

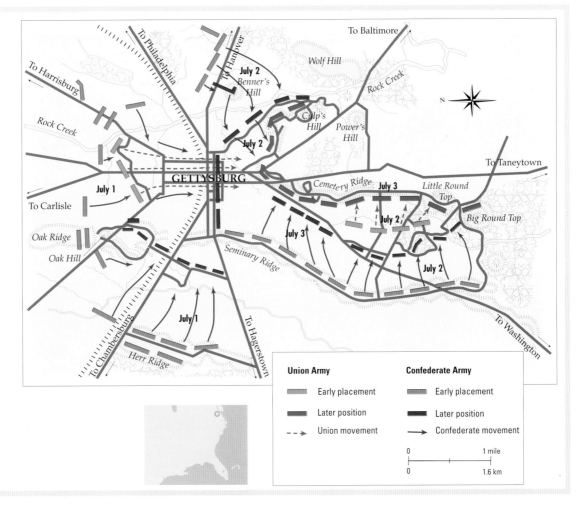

GETTYSBURG

The sacrifices made on the battlefield at Gettysburg continue to touch the nation, and its ground is revered. Cemetery Hill was the central position of the Union forces—and it is here that any visit to the battlefield should begin.

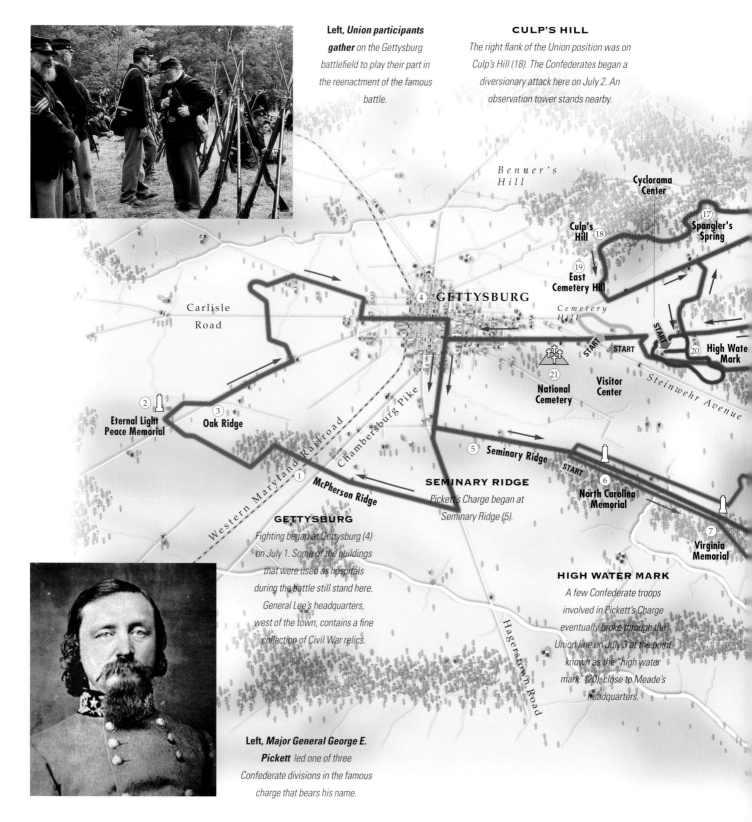

Left, *Union participants gather* on the Gettysburg battlefield to play their part in the reenactment of the famous battle.

CULP'S HILL

The right flank of the Union position was on Culp's Hill (18). The Confederates began a diversionary attack here on July 2. An observation tower stands nearby.

Benner's Hill

Cyclorama Center

17 Spangler's Spring

Culp's Hill 18

19 East Cemetery Hill

Cemetery Hill

4 GETTYSBURG

START

START

START

20 High Water Mark

Carlisle Road

21 National Cemetery

Visitor Center

Steinwehr Avenue

2 Eternal Light Peace Memorial

3 Oak Ridge

Chambersburg Pike

5 Seminary Ridge

START

6 North Carolina Memorial

Western Maryland Railroad

1 McPherson Ridge

SEMINARY RIDGE

Pickett's Charge began at Seminary Ridge (5).

7 Virginia Memorial

GETTYSBURG

Fighting began at Gettysburg (4) on July 1. Some of the buildings that were used as hospitals during the battle still stand here. General Lee's headquarters, west of the town, contains a fine collection of Civil War relics.

Hagerstown Road

HIGH WATER MARK

A few Confederate troops involved in Pickett's Charge eventually broke through the Union line on July 3 at the point known as the "high water mark" (20), close to Meade's headquarters.

Left, *Major General George E. Pickett* led one of three Confederate divisions in the famous charge that bears his name.

CEMETERY RIDGE

Cemetery Hill leads south to Cemetery Ridge—the central position of the Northern forces. The Visitor Center is here, along with a Cyclorama Center featuring a famous painting by Paul Philippoteaux, and the National Civil War Museum displaying over 200 exhibits. The National Cemetery, to the north, contains many of the dead from the battle, and marks the spot where President Lincoln delivered his famous Gettysburg Address.

Left, *Section of Paul Philippoteaux's renowned cyclorama* of the Battle of Gettysburg showing a field hospital.

GETTING THERE

LOCATION: *Gettysburg, Pennsylvania.*

VISITOR INFORMATION: *Gettysburg National Military Park, Gettysburg, PA 17325.*

TELEPHONE: *717-334-1124*

DIRECTIONS: *The Visitor Center is south of Gettysburg on Routes 15 and 134. A self-guided auto tour, as well as several walks, can be followed around the battlefield.*

TOUR DISTANCE: *Driving tour 23 miles (37 km); Walking tour route 1 1mile (1.5 km); walking tour route 3 9 miles (14.5 km); walking tour route 3 ½ mile (0.8 km).*

LITTLE ROUND TOP

The Confederates launched an assault on Little Round Top (11)—the left flank of the Union position—on July 2, but were repulsed thanks to quick action in getting reinforcements by Meade's chief engineer, Brigadier General Gouverneur K. Warren.

DEVIL'S DEN

The rocks and crevices of Devil's Den (10) were well used by Confederate sharpshooters.

Key

③	Battlefield tour stop
START	Starting point
⌂	Monument
✝	Cemetery
▨	Driving tour route
▨	Walking tour route 1
▨	Walking tour route 2
▨	Walking tour route 3

EISENHOWER NATIONAL HISTORIC SITE

Also of interest to visitors may be the Eisenhower National Historic Site—the retirement home used by the former president. This lies to the west of the battlefield.

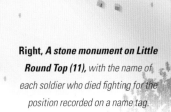

Right, *A stone monument on Little Round Top (11),* with the name of each soldier who died fighting for the position recorded on a name tag.

EUROPE

Nowhere is the soil of battle more sodden with conflict than northwestern Europe.

Two world wars have been fought over it, churning it into a sea of mud and bodies.

The trenches of the Western Front snaked through Belgium and France, and then just 30 years later, the Allies fought Nazism across the same landscape.

Even Napoleon fought his final battle in the same locale, his glorious cavalry being dragged down by the rain and mud of Belgium.

FIGHTING FOR A KINGDOM

Above, *William of Normandy* *surveys his troops disembarking from their ships onto the English shore.*

Left, *the traditional representation* *of the death of Harold, recorded on the Bayeux Tapestry. Legend has it that he was killed by an arrow in the eye, but some contemporary accounts report that he died when cut to pieces by Norman knights.*

THE GREAT BATTLE that decided England's fate—whether it was to be ruled by Saxon or Norman French kings—was fought on a hill north of Hastings, in southeastern England. Today, almost 1,000 years later, the hill is cloaked in long green grass, with trees and marshy land at its base. On the ridge stand the beautiful ruins of Battle Abbey.

On October 14, 1066, the hill was crowded with men in armor swinging swords, maces, and spears in a desperate struggle that lasted almost a whole day. For William the Bastard, Duke of Normandy, this was a righteous crusade against the Saxon king Harold II, who had broken a sacred promise to him. There was no turning back for William and his men. They were on foreign territory, and if they failed they would be hunted down and massacred. For Harold, it was the second challenge to his authority in a month. He had won the first, and his victorious warriors would not give ground before these new invaders. Neither side

In January 1066, King Edward the Confessor died with no obvious successor. Immediately, Harold Godwinson, Earl of Wessex and commander of the King's army, proclaimed himself King.

However, William, Duke of Normandy and cousin to Edward the Confessor, had himself expected to inherit the English throne, especially as two years earlier Harold had promised to support his claim. William thus regarded Harold as a usurper.

Through the spring and summer of 1066, William prepared to invade England, building ships and recruiting soldiers. Pope Alexander II sent his blessing, and the enterprise acquired the spirit of a crusade.

Besides William, Harold faced other opponents to his crown, and on September 25, 1066 he defeated an army led by his own brother Tostig and Harold Sigurdssen (Hardraade) of Norway at the battle of Stamford Bridge, near York.

Meanwhile, William set sail from St. Valéry-sur-Somme. His invasion fleet landed at Pevensey in East Sussex at the end of September, and Harold quickly marched his army south down the length of England to confront him on October 14 at the site subsequently named Battle.

would back down, and both armies were prepared to fight to exhaustion.

Great seal of William the Conqueror.
The mantle of "Conqueror" was assigned to William of Normandy by historians after his success at Hastings in 1066.

STRONG POSITION

William brought about 7,000 supporters to the battlefield of Hastings, including 2,000 mounted Norman warriors who fought from horseback with long shields, lances, and swords. His other warriors included foot soldiers, mostly from Normandy and Brittany, but also from other parts of France, such as Aquitaine. They fought mainly without armor, and carried shields, spears, bows, and slings.

Harold faced William with a similar-sized army of mounted armored warriors and foot soldiers armed with spears and bows. At the core of his army was his loyal elite personal body-guard, known as housecarls, who were noted for fighting with long two-handed axes. Some historians think that Harold's men, having defeated a Norwegian invasion at Stamford Bridge in the north of England just three weeks earlier and then making the long march south, must have been exhausted. But soldiers' spirits are always raised by victory; it seems likely that the troops were hungry for more success and the accompanying loot that a medieval battlefield provided.

Harold was an astute military commander and knew that victory often depended on selecting the right battleground. Harold chose a strong defensive position at the top of Senlac

LEADERSHIP

Command in a medieval battle was a highly personal undertaking. Your warriors could see you and observe your performance in the face of violence, and the best commanders were those who fought bravely with their warriors in the front rank. If a commander lost his nerve and fled, his army would quickly follow him. William of Normandy was a model front-line commander. Writing shortly after the Battle of Hastings, the chronicler William of Poitiers described the duke in battle:

Three horses were killed under him. Three times he leapt undismayed to the ground and put paid to the man who had slaughtered his horse .... With savage sword-blows, brooking no delay, he cleft shields, helmets, hauberks [mail shirts]. With his own shield he struck a number of the enemy. His soldiers, some of them wounded, took new courage when they saw him fighting on foot. Some, who were weak from loss of blood, leant on their shields and fought on manfully; others, who could do no more, shouted to their comrades and made gestures to them, encouraging them to follow where the duke had led, lest victory should slip out of their hands.

From THE BAYEUX TAPESTRY AND THE NORMAN INVASION, *translated by Lewis Thorpe (The Folio Society, 1973).*

Chaos at the heart of the final Norman attack on the Saxon shield wall at the top of Senlac Hill, reenacted on the site by medieval living history societies during a recent anniversary of the Battle of Hastings.

Hill, near the present-day village of Battle, and waited for the Normans to attack. His elite warriors dismounted and formed a tight line, holding their shields to create a wall of wood and metal against their enemies' weapons.

William knew that the Saxon position was strong, but he had no choice of what action to take. If he ignored the Saxon army he would have to abandon his claim to the area, and within days his troops would become disorganized and short of supplies. He had to attack, and he had to attack up Senlac Hill. The full challenge of his situation can only be appreciated by standing on the marshy ground at the bottom of the slope and looking up to the top of the ridge. The wall of soldiers must have been a daunting sight for William's men. The only possible tactic was to break the shield wall by provoking some of the Saxons into a rash attack.

Left, *Medieval mail shirt.*
Mail, made of tiny, interlocking iron rings, was an effective form of armor against the swords of medieval warriors.

Below, *Imaginative reconstruction of the fighting at the top of Senlac Hill,* *showing a mounted Norman knight leading a desperate attack against the Saxon shield wall. (Painting by R. Caton Woodville.)*

PHYSICAL EXHAUSTION

William ordered his archers to begin shooting high in the air so that their arrows would fall on top of the Saxon army. But the Saxons were accustomed to such a strategy and simply raised their shields higher. Waves of Normans then assaulted the Saxons in hand-to-hand fighting—but the Saxon wall did not break. The Norman warriors were forced back, their limbs exhausted by the exertion of wielding swords and shields in close combat. At one point, the Norman army feared that William had been killed, and he was obliged to remove his helmet and show his face to restore his men's spirits.

Neither side was yielding. With frequent pauses for the soldiers to gather breath and revive their declining muscle power, the battle dragged on into the afternoon. It was then that the Saxons made a fatal error. Perhaps under the impression that the

Scene from the Bayeux Tapestry, showing Harold, Earl of Wessex swearing an oath to William, Duke of Normandy, in which he promises to support William's claim to the English throne. When Harold later broke the oath by proclaiming himself king, William felt justified in challenging his authority.

Normans were too exhausted to continue, and that one final charge would defeat them, some of the Saxon line broke away and charged down hill. It was the opportunity William had been waiting for. He rallied some of his cavalrymen and turned on the vulnerable breakaway soldiers. The Norman horsemen cut the running soldiers down.

The Saxon line was shrinking, and William ordered one more assault. He aimed at the center of the line with his mounted warriors. They broke into the circle of housecarls surrounding Harold and, in bitter hand-to-hand fighting, reached Harold himself. The Saxon king was struck down, and with his death, the battle was decided. His army fell back and eventually disintegrated; as night came, Harold's men fled into the dark to escape the pursuing Normans. William the Bastard of Normandy had gained a kingdom and a new sobriquet: William the Conqueror.

HASTINGS

ASTINGS IS RARE in being an almost perfectly preserved medieval battlefield. Its importance in the history of England ensured that the site was protected from an early stage. William had an abbey built in order to thank God for divine support in the battle. Its altar marked the exact spot where Harold fell. This final struggle was a bitter contest, emblematic of the close physical combat that characterized medieval warfare.

According to the chronicler Guy of Amiens, William rode forward with three of his most trustworthy warriors: Eustace; Hugh, heir to Ponthieu; and Giffard. They pushed through the crowd of fighting men to get close to where Harold and his elite warriors were fiercely contesting the ridge with the Normans. Soon Harold was surrounded, and exhausted by the long day's struggle, he had little energy to resist their attack.

William thrust his lance into Harold's shield, disabling his defense. Eustace swung his sword with one mighty blow and

Portrait of William, Duke of Normandy, hunting with hawks: a detail from the Bayeux Tapestry. The tapestry was commissioned to celebrate William's conquest of England.

cut off Harold's head. Hugh disemboweled the king with his spear, and Giffard sank a deep cut into his thigh, severing his leg. This was the brutal way of medieval warfare—complete annihilation of one's enemy. The body was then trampled and lost in the fierce fighting that must have broken out when the Saxon knights witnessed the death of their beloved leader, and sought vengeance. It was only with great difficulty that William found the mangled body of Harold in the darkness after the battle was over, and had it buried on the seashore.

The less violent story of Harold's being struck down by an arrow in his eye occurs in the work of later medieval historians, and maintained credibility because an image seeming to represent this appears in the Bayeux Tapestry. The tapestry was completed shortly after the battle, and is a remarkably accurate record of William's invasion of England, including the details of building the boats and gathering materials for the fighting.

PLAN OF BATTLE

In an effort to check the Norman invasion, a line of Saxon foot soldiers stood along the ridge at the top of Senlac Hill. The Norman forces were arrayed in three main groups at the bottom of the hill, with William and his mounted Normans in the center, and his Breton and French allies on either side of him. The Normans attacked uphill. Each army numbered about 7,000 men. The hard-fought battle lasted all day, and in such a long and desperate confrontation, the numbers of dead and wounded would have been undoubtedly high.

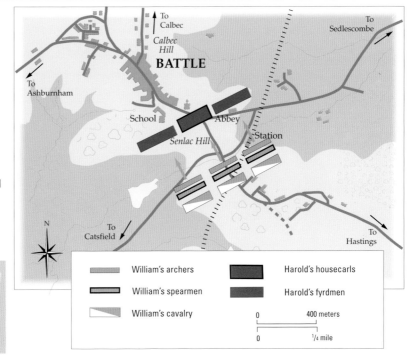

William's archers
William's spearmen
William's cavalry
Harold's housecarls
Harold's fyrdmen

HASTINGS

Hastings' well preserved battlefield is focused around the Abbey that William the Conqueror ordered to be built to commemorate his victory. Today, the Abbey dominates the village that has built up around it and taken its name from that fateful day in October 1066—Battle. Within the Abbey's walls visitors can watch a film and then recapture the excitement of medieval warfare by taking an audio walking tour around Senlac Hill, site of the Battle of Hastings.

Above, *The ruins of Battle Abbey (6),* built in 1094 and extended throughout the Middle Ages. The Saxons were slowly forced back from the ridge to this ground under repeated Norman assaults. The altar stood on the spot where King Harold fell.

Left, *Saxon and Norman warriors* clash in single combat. The Saxon has his back to us. Both warriors wear mail armor typical of the period, and carry kite-shaped shields that would allow them to fight from horseback.

Battle Abbey

The Harold Stone

Battle Abbey School

Position of Harold's right flank

START

Key

③   Battlefield tour stop

START   Starting point

   Battlefield tour route

   Abbey tour route

Right, *A plaque (5)* marks the spot where Harold was fatally struck down during the Battle of Hastings.

Above, *The ridge along the top of Senlac Hill (1),* where Harold positioned his Saxon army.

**Valley between
Norman and Saxon positions**
④

GETTING THERE

LOCATION: *Battle, East Sussex, U.K.*

VISITOR INFORMATION: *English Heritage, 23 Savile Row, London W1X 1AB.*

TELEPHONE: *01424 773792*

DIRECTIONS: *By road from London to Royal Tunbridge Wells and then A21 to Battle; parking lot near site. Train from London Charing Cross or London Bridge direct to Battle station.*

TOUR DISTANCE: *1¼ miles (3 km).*

②
**Bottom of
Senlac Hill**

③
Marshland

Below, *Marshy ground at the bottom of the hill (2),* where William gathered his warriors into three groups; Bretons stood near the present-day pond.

BATTLE FOR A CROWN

Above, *In an imagined scene, Richard, Duke of York* (left)
plucks a white rose to represent his forces in the coming civil war,
while the Duke of Somerset plucks a red rose to represent the
House of Lancaster.

Left, *Artist's romantic interpretation of the final clash at*
Bosworth Field, *when Richard III rode toward Henry Tudor: two*
contenders for the crown pitted in single combat. In reality, Richard
was cut down before he could reach Henry, when his horse stumbled.

THE SECOND MOST IMPORTANT BATTLE in the history of England
was fought in marshy fields in the county of Leicestershire. Like
the Battle of Hastings, the conflict created a new royal dynasty,
one of the most famous in British history: the Tudors. The hill still
stands where a king was crowned, and below are the fields where
another king's crown was lost. This was the battle immortalized by
William Shakespeare, whose desperate King Richard III cries, "A horse!
A horse! My kingdom for a horse!"

WARS OF THE ROSES

Bosworth Field was the culmination of a series of campaigns and civil
wars in the late fifteenth century known, since Shakespeare's time, as
the Wars of the Roses. Wealthy families fought to claim the throne
of England. After nearly 30 years of strife, Henry Tudor, Earl of
Richmond, landed in August, 1485 at Milford Haven in Wales with an
army of 3,000 French mercenaries. Soldiers from Wales and the west of
England joined his army, and Henry marched into central England to
confront Richard III with a force of about 5,000 men. Richard's army
was between two and three times larger; much of his military support
came from the Stanley family.

The Wars of the Roses, where the
white rose of the House of York
was pitted against the red rose of
the Lancastrians, began with the
madness of the Lancastrian king
Henry VI. He had lost control of
the country, and Richard, Duke of
York, was elected Protector by
Parliament in 1454. However,
Henry's wife, Queen Margaret
contrived to have Richard
dismissed, and, with the Duke of
Somerset, took command.

Richard responded by rallying his
supporters, including Richard
Neville, Earl of Warwick. The
lines of civil war were drawn.

The Yorkists were the first to
triumph at the Battle of Towton in
1461, when Richard's son became
King Edward IV.

Ten years later, Warwick
changed sides and led an
invasion from France. Edward
was briefly forced to flee, but he
later rallied to kill Warwick and
rout the Lancastrians at the
Battle of Barnet in April, 1471.

In 1483 Edward died and was
succeeded by his 13-year-old
son, but the boy was killed by
Edward's brother Richard, Duke
of Gloucester, who became
Richard III.

Two years later, Henry Tudor
contested Richard's claim to the
throne at the Battle of Bosworth
Field, the closing battle of the
Wars of the Roses.

Richard camped his army on Ambion Hill near the village of Dadlington. Sir William Stanley and Lord Thomas Stanley were in control of a separate force. Henry Tudor took the offensive and led his army across the waterlogged fields between Shenton and Dadlington.

Armies at this time consisted of armored warriors, or knights, who usually headed battle groups of supporters, including foot soldiers armed with polearms—blades attached to the end of poles—and bows. Gunpowder was also used in primitive cannons and handguns. Battle groups faced each other, and the knights were the target. An armored foot soldier, carrying a handgun, aimed to attack a

knight, because if the knight fell, as commander and paymaster of the battle group, the rest of his battle group would often disintegrate.

As the two forces drew closer, Richard ordered his men forward, but his left wing—commanded by the Stanleys—refused to move. The Stanleys then decided that their best opportunity lay with Henry, and they switched sides. Richard was fatally outnumbered, but not lacking in personal bravery. Battle-ax in hand, he led a desperate charge down Ambion Hill toward Henry, in a bid to seize victory single-handedly or die like a king. His boldness was not rewarded. As he was cut down, his crown fell from his helmet. According to legend, it rolled into a bush; it was retrieved, and placed on Henry's head on Crown Hill at Stoke Golding. A new dynasty held sway in England.

*Above, **Armored men-at-arms and an archer**, typical of those who fought at Bosworth Field, wear a mixture of mail and plate armor.*

*Below, **Cannons of the type used during the Wars of the Roses**. They were far less powerful than the cannons of later centuries, but the sight and sound of them exploding into action was nonetheless unnerving to advancing warriors.*

THE REAL BATTLEFIELD

Recently dicovered evidence contradicts the traditional view of the Battle of Bosworth Field. Rather than being fought on the slopes of Ambion Hill, it was apparently fought nearer the village of Dadlington, on flat ground between Ambion Hill and Crown Hill, around what is now known as Fen Meadow. The discovery of medieval weapons and pieces of armor near Stoke Golding reinforces this view. Acording to new findings, the battle was fought around the marshy ground of Fen Meadow, which both sides tried to avoid. Richard's right wing advanced against Henry's main army on the west side of the marsh. Clouds of arrows were exchanged before the two sides met in

Below, *Padded and studded brigantine,* helmet, gauntlets, and mail armor ensured that foot soldiers were well protected from both swords and arrows.

Left, *Sallet with visor,* typical German-style helmet worn by armored warriors during the Wars of the Roses.

hand-to-hand combat. The Stanleys were located on the east side of the marsh, and it seems likely that Richard then led a direct attack on Henry in order to prevent these two forces from converging. But the charge lay through the marsh, which must have affected its impact. Richard was unhorsed, and one grisly account has him caught in the mire by a Welshman, who crushed his helmet with a halberd until his brains oozed out.

MEDIEVAL COMBAT

It is not difficult to imagine the rich panoply of medieval combat, with knights charging on armored horses beneath the glorious pennants that bear their heraldic colors, while groups of archers and foot soldiers stand to one side, contributing their fighting skills when needed.

This is the way that numerous movies have represented medieval warfare, but recent research suggests an alternative vision of medieval battle.

Later periods of warfare in which rows of similarly armed soldiers fought alongside each other gave rise to the view that in earlier times archers and foot soldiers fought separately from knights. But at battles such as Bosworth Field, this was seemingly not the case, in light of the social forces that brought the warriors to the battlefield. Soldiers were not recruited, as in later times, but were obliged to serve the lord who employed them on his land. They were his servants and laborers, and as such would be led by him into battle to fight by his side. A knight would frequently show up for battle with his friends and family, arrayed as men-at-arms in armor and on horseback; and his employees, equipped with spears, axes, and bows, to serve as foot soldiers. The men had a vested interest in defending their lord, because without him there would be no employment, and their future would be unsure. Thus the servants were always on hand to tend their lord and protect him. They fought together, and died together.

It seems likely that Bosworth Field was contested by myriad small gangs, bonded by social ties. Each gang would locate an opposing gang, and seek to destroy the leading knight. At the time of Bosworth Field, guns had become important, and each knight probably employed one soldier to carry a handgun. This was used like a massive shotgun to blast the opposing armored knight and cause his less well-armored servants to flee the field. Such battles could be complicated and confusing, and Bosworth Field was no exception. The outcome hung in the balance for some time, additionally prolonged by the Stanleys' political game of wait-and-see.

DEATH OF A KING

Polydore Vergil is the main, near-contemporary source of information about the Battle of Bosworth Field, and his account is probably based on the reports of eyewitnesses. Here, he describes Richard III's courageous actions in battle:

All inflamed with ire, he [Richard] strick his horse with the spurs . . . . Henry perceived King Richard come upon him, and because all his hope was then in valiancy of arms, he received him with great courage. King Richard at the first brunt killed certain, overthrew Henry's standard, together with William Brandon the standard bearer, and matched also with John Cheney a man of much fortitude, far exceeding the common sort, who encountered with him as he came, but the king with great force drove him to the ground, making way with weapon on every side. But yet Henry abode the brunt longer than ever his own soldiers would have weened, who were almost out of hope of victory, when as lo William Stanley with three thousand men came to the rescue . . . and King Richard alone was killed fighting manfully in the thickest press of his enemies.

Quoted in THE WARS OF THE ROSES
by J.R. Lander
(Sutton, 1990)

Henry Tudor, painted as King Henry VII. His victory at Bosworth Field led to the elevation of one of the most famous royal dynasties in English history.

BOSWORTH FIELD

Above, *Rolling hills and open countryside* *make a trip to the battlefield of Bosworth Field a pleasant place to relive history.*

THE MARSHY FIELDS that played such an important role in the Battle of Bosworth Field have now been drained, and the open meadows replaced by hedged fields. A railroad track cuts across the land, but good views of the battlefield can still be had from Ambion Hill and Crown Hill.

The evolution of landscape has contributed to the fervent academic debate about the location of the battle. The area around Ambion Hill and Crown Hill has changed so much since the fifteenth century that the only topographical feature of the battle that was ever certain—the marshy ground—has long disappeared. Land improvement, enclosure, canal-building, and the advent of the railways have all taken their toll on this historical site.

It is known that adequate drainage of this area would not have taken place until Tudor times, so the area between the two armies before they took up their battle positions was one of bog, marsh, and waste. Those who fought in the battle would have known the area between the villages of Shenton, Sutton Cheney, Stoke Golding, and Dadlington as Redmoors, Redmoor Plain, or Bosworth Heath.

PLAN OF BATTLE

Little is known about the order of battle at Bosworth Field. Tradition has Richard's army arrayed on the slopes of Ambion Hill, but the current view is that Richard's main force (under Norfolk) confronted Henry's army (commanded by Oxford) on the flat land now known as Fen Meadow. The Stanleys occupied a position on the other side of the marshy field nearest Dadlington. Henry's army initially numbered 5,000 and Richard's was considerably larger, but when the Stanleys changed sides, they brought at least 3,000 men to Henry's side. The battle lasted approximately two hours, with possibly 1,000 slain on Richard's side, and 100 on Henry's.

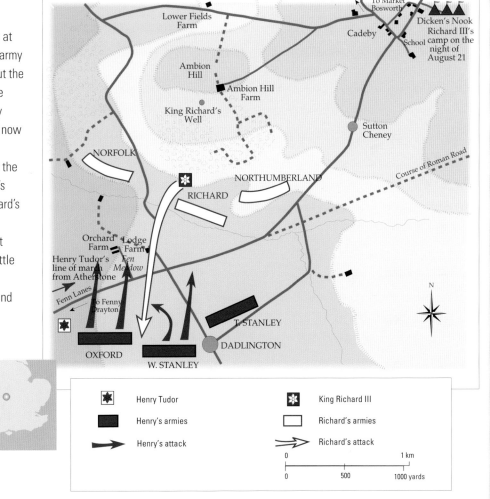

77

BOSWORTH FIELD

AMBION HILL FARM HOSTS a battlefield center that relates the story of the Battle of Bosworth Field and guides vistors toward battlefield trails with interpretative display panels. The battlefield center has chosen to promote the school of thought that believes the battle took place to the west of Ambion Hill, around Fen Meadow, rather than to to the southwest of Ambion Hill. Several parking lots are dotted around the battlefield area for ease of access to the trails.

Above, *A re-created line of men-at-arms,* raising their polearms to attack as the foot soldiers at Bosworth Field would have done. Usually known as billmen, they fought in close formation and could efficiently repel assault by knights on horseback.

Below, *Crown Hill, near Stoke Golding,* where Richard's crown was placed on Henry's head.

Shenton

Viewpoint of battle between Oxford and Norfolk

④

New Barn

White Moors (Parking Lot)

FEN MEADOW

Bisected by the Roman road of Fenn Lanes, Fen Meadow (3) was the area of marshy land where it is now believed the main battle took place.

Me

Crown Hill

N

Left, *King Richard's Well.*
The king reputedly took a drink from this well before the charge in which he lost his life. It is marked by a stone pyramid erected in his memory.

Above, *Ambion Hill* is the traditional location of Richard III's army. The battlefield center here marks the start of a signposted walking trail.

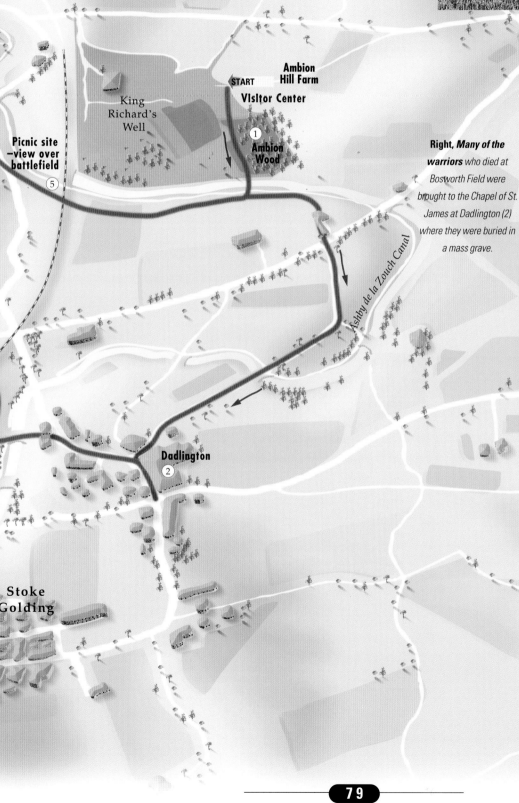

Right, *Many of the warriors* who died at Bosworth Field were brought to the Chapel of St. James at Dadlington (2) where they were buried in a mass grave.

Ambion
Hill Farm
START
Visitor Center

King
Richard's
Well

Picnic site
—view over
battlefield
(5)

(1)
**Ambion
Wood**

Ashby de la Zouch Canal

Dadlington
(2)

**Stoke
Golding**

GETTING THERE

LOCATION:
Dadlington, Leicestershire.

VISITOR INFORMATION:
Bosworth Battlefield Centre, Sutton Cheney, Market Bosworth, Leicestershire, CV1B 0AD.

TELEPHONE:
01455 290429

DIRECTIONS:
M69 from Coventry or Leicester, then A447 to Hinckley and Dadlington; parking lot on Ambion Hill. Train to Leicester; nearest station is Burbage in Hinckley.

TOUR DISTANCE: $5\frac{1}{2}$ miles (8.5 km).

NAPOLEON'S FINAL CHALLENGE

Above, **Napoleon Bonaparte**, commander of the French army at Waterloo. His spectacular return from exile galvanized his supporters, and there was a real belief that he could defeat the armies arrayed against him. (Painting by Delaroche.)

Left, **Hougoumont farmhouse** was successfully defended by the Allies on their right wing, and remained out of Napoleon's reach throughout the battle.

APOLEON WAS THE CAESAR OF HIS DAY: a totalitarian ruler who dreamed of uniting Europe under his command. He was an idealist who spent much of his time designing regulations to improve people's lives—but first he had to conquer them. In 1812, Napoleon or his relatives ruled much of Europe, including France, the Netherlands, Italy, Spain, Germany, Austria, and Poland. He had marched to Moscow, and he had threatened Britain with invasion. Two years later, his empire was in tatters and he was a prisoner on the Mediterranean island of Elba.

In 1815, however, Napoleon escaped. For one hundred days, the emperor was back in France and back in command. Napoleon was a charismatic leader in the mold of Alexander the Great. He believed in simple aggressive tactics that targeted the heart of the enemy. His troops were arranged in columns; they cheered their emperor and aimed to break the enemy with the speed and courage of their advance. Napoleon

BACKGROUND TO BATTLE

On March 1, 1815 Napoleon landed at Cannes in France, having escaped from exile on the island of Elba. From Cannes, he marched to Paris and resumed control of the French army.

The European Allies responded to this development by declaring Napoleon an outlaw. By June 1, the Allies had raised a formidable array of armies to oppose him: in Belgium were Wellington's 95,000 British and Dutch, and Field Marshal Blücher's 124,000 Prussians; 210,000 Germans lay along the Rhine frontier; 75,000 Austrians were in Italy; and a Russian army of 167,000 was moving westward.

Napoleon decided to try to defeat the Allies one at a time, and struck northward into Belgium to deal with Wellington and the Prussians before they could join forces. On June 16, Napoleon attacked the Prussians, led by Blücher, at Ligny, and the Prussians reeled back.

Meanwhile, Napoleon's Field Marshal Ney battled a British vanguard at Quatre-Bras. Napoleon wanted Ney's support at Ligny, but the British held out, enabling Wellington to gather his forces at Waterloo.

Blücher retreated to Wavre and was ready to join Wellington at Waterloo, where Napoleon had turned his attention to the British.

raised such an army to confront his enemies in Belgium, near the village of Waterloo.

WELLINGTON

Two powerful armies stood in Napoleon's way. One was primarily British, commanded by the Duke of Wellington, the other was Prussian, under Field Marshal Blücher. Wellington was a veteran commander who had led British forces against the French in Spain, but he had never directly opposed Napoleon on the battlefield.

Wellington was a cooler character than Napoleon, and he put great trust in practicality. For example, he was a master of the landscape of battle. In Spain, he had perfected the technique of positioning his men on the reverse side of a slope, so that the enemy would not know the true strength of his deployment. At close quarters, his soldiers would rise, fire one volley, and charge with bayonets extended. In his experience this had always been enough to disperse the French.

At Waterloo, Wellington chose the battlefield. He commanded an army of mixed nationality, including British, Dutch, Belgian, and German. The center of his position was

Below, *The Battle of Quatre-Bras,* *a preliminary confrontation in which British soldiers held off the French, giving Wellington time to organize his troops at Waterloo. Here, the 28th Foot form a square to fight off the French cavalry, a tactic later used successfully at Waterloo. (Painting by Lady Butler.)*

Above, *Arthur Wellesley, Duke of Wellington,* *also known as the "Iron Duke," was a formidable commander who had distinguished himself on the battlefield in India, Denmark, and Spain before Waterloo.*

farmland, and he placed the majority of his British regiments on the reverse slope of a low plateau running along the Ohain Road. He used farmhouses (Papelotte, Hougoumont, and La Haie-Sainte) as fortified positions ahead of his flanks and center to break up an enemy advance. It was a defensive position, because Wellington hoped to hold the French until his ally, the Prussian General Blücher, could arrive with his Prussian soldiers.

If the strategy was typical of Wellington, Napoleon's attack was also characteristic. After a massive artillery bombardment of the Allied lines, his troops advanced noisily and determinedly toward them at noon. It had rained the previous night and the ground was heavy with mud that clung to the soldiers' boots. Nevertheless, the French advance was successful. Papelotte was captured, and by 4:00 P.M.

Left, *The Duke of Wellington* and his staff officers cross the Bidossa River from Spain to France in 1813, the culmination of his successful campaign in the Peninsular War. Many of Wellington's victories were due to his mastery of terrain, and he would later employ this skill at Waterloo to defeat Napoleon.

the Allied line was forced back. The French were so sure that the British could be broken before the arrival of the Prussians that Field Marshal Ney, one of Napoleon's leading generals, took it upon himself to order a massive French cavalry attack. Napoleon later commented that it had been launched an hour too soon.

DEATH OF A GENTLEMAN

Charles O'Neil served in the 28th (North Gloucestershire) Regiment, and fought under Wellington's command both in Spain and at Waterloo. Here, he describes the death of Sir William Ponsonby, the commander of three regiments of cavalry, at the height of the battle:

He [Ponsonby] led his brigade against the Polish lancers, and took two hundred prisoners; but riding on in advance of his troops, he entered a newly ploughed field, when his horse stuck in the mire, and he found it impossible to proceed. At this instant, a body of lancers rode up. Sir William saw that his fate was inevitable. He took out his watch and a picture, and desired some one near to send them to his wife. A moment after, he fell, pierced with seven lance wounds.

From THE MILITARY ADVENTURES OF CHARLES O'NEIL, *1851*

Dutch red-coated lancers fighting the French at Waterloo.
This painting by Lalauze captures the magnificence of the uniformed soldiers of this period, although heavy rain on the eve of Waterloo, and the resultant mud, must have diminished their splendor.

BRITISH SQUARES

As always when threatened by French cavalry, the British and their allies formed squares—regiments raised their muskets with bayonets attached, creating a hedgehog-like shield against the attacking horses. The majority of the squares formed behind the ridge of the plateau, out of the line of cannon fire. The slope reduced the impetus of the French cavalry, and, unsupported by artillery, it could do little to break the squares. The French horsemen slowed down and were raked by British musket fire. Again and again the cavalry attacked, but the squares held fast and the French eventually gave up.

At 6:00 P.M. the Prussians were nearing the battlefield. Napoleon concentrated on this threat, while Ney rallied his men and led another assault on the British line and captured

*Above, **A soldier of the 69th Foot**, loading his India Pattern flintlock musket, more affectionately known as the Brown Bess musket.*

La Haie-Sainte. Wellington rode among his men, ordering them to hold the line. With the Prussians momentarily in check, Napoleon decided to make one last effort against Wellington and sent forward his elite forces, the Old Guard.

Ney was in command, and led the Old Guard against Wellington's right flank, still covered by Hougoumont, instead of directly against the weakened center. Allied artillery from behind the farmhouse reduced the impact of the French advance. The British refused to move and fought a furious firefight. Eventually, the Old Guard faltered. Elsewhere on the battlefield, at Plancenoit, Blücher and his Prussians renewed their attack. It was after 8:00 P.M. when Wellington ordered a general advance, and the French line collapsed. The battle was over—Napoleon was beaten.

*Below, **Charge of the Scots Greys at Waterloo**: one of the most heroic moments of the battle and, although initially successful, the British cavalry suffered in a counterattack—an example of how the battle swung back and forth for most of the day. (Painting by Lady Butler.)*

WATERLOO

A<small>N IDEA OF WHAT</small> it was like to be a soldier on the battle-field of Waterloo is conveyed in the memoirs ascribed to Thomas Howell of the 71st Highland Regiment.

Howell complained about the ceaseless rain that tormented him during the night before combat. French artillery pounded his lines sporadically throughout the morning. At noon, he and his comrades were ordered to advance to their part of the ridge, which they were instructed to hold. They lay down on the grass, and many fell asleep instantly, so tired were they after marching for two days.

"I slept sound for some time while the cannonballs, plunging in amongst us, killed a great many," Howell recalled. "I

was suddenly awakened. A ball struck the ground a little below me, turned me heels-over-head, broke my musket in pieces and killed a lad at my side." Howell lay stunned for some time while French artillery killed sixty of his comrades.

At 2:00 P.M., the 71st were approached by French lancers, and quickly formed a defensive square. Smoke and noise were everywhere, and Howell could see very little, apart from men falling all around him. The 71st then kept in square formation for most of the afternoon until Wellington ordered them to advance. "This was our last effort; nothing could impede us," says Howell. "The whole of the enemy retired, leaving their guns and ammunition and every other thing behind."

PLAN OF BATTLE

At the peak of battle, at 4:00 P.M., Wellington's Anglo-Dutch forces were forced back behind the ridge of the Ohain Road. Pockets of Allies at the three farmhouses of Hougoumont, La Haie-Sainte, and Papelotte maintained resistance to the French, slowing their advance. To the east, the Prussians were advancing. Wellington's forces numbered about 68,000 and Napoleon's about 72,000.

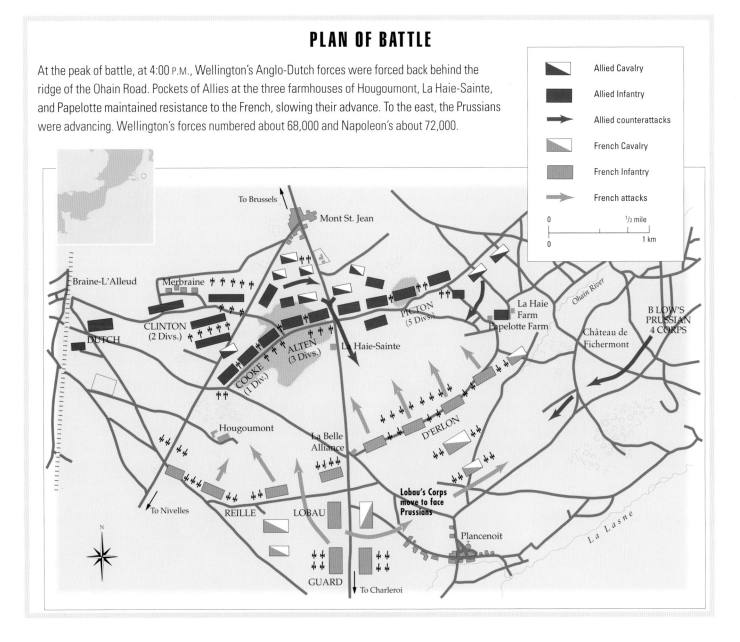

WATERLOO

THE FIELD OF WATERLOO today is farmland, just as it was during the battle that made it famous. It is dominated by the giant Lion Mound, and mounting the 226 steps of this monument gives a spectacular view of the entire battlefield. The 42,000 cubic yards of earth excavated to make the mound have, however, altered the profile of the land in the center of the battlefield. On the day of the battle, this area saw some of the fiercest fighting.

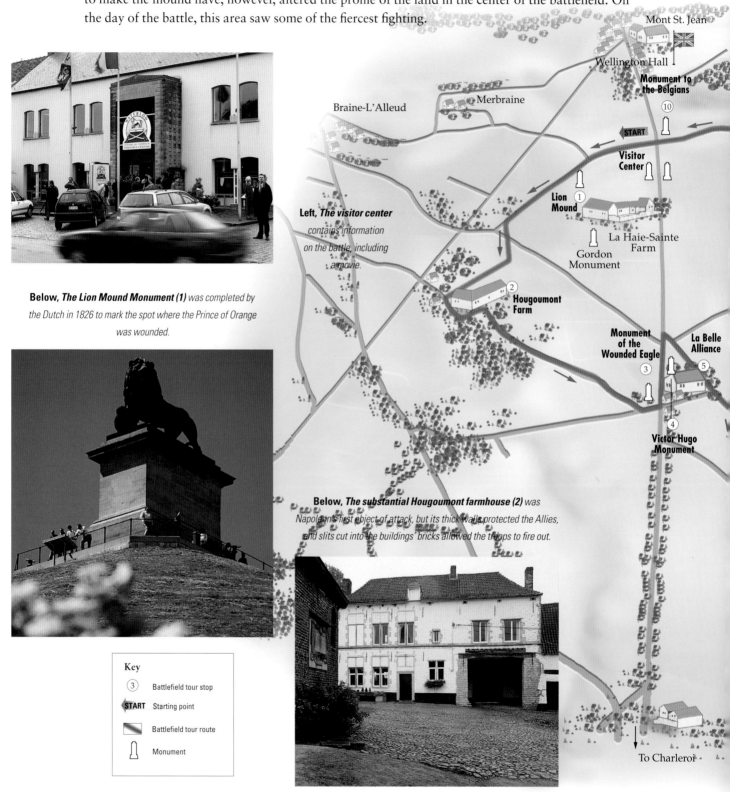

*Left, **The visitor center** contains information on the battle, including a movie.*

Below, *The Lion Mound Monument (1)* *was completed by the Dutch in 1826 to mark the spot where the Prince of Orange was wounded.*

Mont St. Jean

Wellington Hall

Monument to the Belgians

Braine-L'Alleud

Merbraine

START

Visitor Center

10

Lion Mound 1

La Haie-Sainte Farm

Gordon Monument

Hougoumont Farm 2

Monument of the Wounded Eagle 3

La Belle Alliance 5

4

Victor Hugo Monument

Below, *The substantial Hougoumont farmhouse (2)* *was Napoleon's first object of attack, but its thick walls protected the Allies, and slits cut into the buildings' bricks allowed the troops to fire out.*

To Charleroi

Key

3 — Battlefield tour stop

START — Starting point

— Battlefield tour route

— Monument

Right, _La Haie-Sainte_ was the fortified farmhouse in the center of Wellington's position. Fiercely defended by Germans and Dutch, it eventually fell to the French after great loss of life.

GETTING THERE

LOCATION: _8 miles (5 km) south of Waterloo, central Belgium._

VISITOR INFORMATION: _Visitor Center, Route du Lion 252-254, B-1420 Braine L'Alleud, Belgium._

TELEPHONE: _2-385-19-12_

DIRECTIONS FROM BRUSSELS: _By car take the Ring 0 on the eastern side until exit 25. By train from Brussels South Central or Brussels North, take train toward Charleroi or Nivelles and alight at Braine-l'Alleud; from there take a bus heading toward Brussels. By bus, from station at Rouppe ask for a bus that stops at the Lion of Waterloo._

TOUR DISTANCE: _6½ miles (10.5 km)._

La Haie Farm

⑨ **Ohain Road**

⑧ **Papelotte Farm**

Château de Fichermont

OHAIN ROAD

Wellington arrayed his army along the line of the Ohain Road (6), sheltering most of the soldiers on the gentle reverse slope of the plateau.

Monument to the Prussians
⑦

La Lasne

⑥ **Plancenoit**

Above, _Near Plancenoit_ is the monument (7) erected in memory of the Prussians who died at the battle.

Right, _The Monument of the Wounded Eagle (3)_ commemorates the last stand of Napoleon's Old Guard.

THE PITY OF WAR

Above, ***The reality of life on the Western Front.*** *Mud and rain transformed the appearance of the Tommy, who improvised his leggings and boots to protect feet from trench rot and other infections.*

Left, ***No-man's-land,*** *the devastated and barbed-wire filled terrain that lay beyond the trenches of the Somme battlefield.*

BACKGROUND TO BATTLE

The costly Battle of the Somme had been intended to serve as a diversion to the bloodshed at Verdun, where, on February 21, 1916, the Germans had begun an assault that led to huge losses among the French Army.

Attacks and counterattacks continued for months and eroded both armies.

Verdun became a symbol of the French sacrifice to protect their nation. They were determined not to let Verdun fall—but it cost them dearly and French morale slumped.

The French needed a British attack in the north to draw some of the German strength away from Verdun.

British commander, General Sir Douglas Haig saw the need for action in the Somme region, and it was planned as a joint Anglo-French attack.

Continuing German assaults at Verdun, however, reduced the number of French troops available and expanded the role of British and Commonwealth soldiers in the Battle of the Somme.

OF ALL THE TERRIBLE BATTLES of World War I, the battle fought beside the River Somme in northern France echoes loudest. On a single horrifying day, the British Army suffered 60,000 casualties, including 19,000 dead. It was the greatest one-day loss in the army's history. Lines of khaki-clad men climbed out of their trenches, walked a few yards into no-man's-land, and were mowed down by German machine guns. This is an image forever linked with World War I.

BOMBARDMENT

In the view of General Sir Douglas Haig, the British commander, the attack could not fail. On July 1, 1916, the advance of the British Fourth Army was preceded by a ferocious bombardment. In the final 65 minutes before zero hour, 224,220 shells were fired and ten massive mines were detonated

wire between the two lines. As soon as the bombardment ceased, German soldiers rushed out of their shelters to man their machine guns and were confronted with the sight of thousands of British soldiers walking toward their positions. It was a massacre. Within an hour, British casualties numbered 30,000.

Haig is often held solely responsible for this disaster, but he was given false reassurances by his subordinates. Reports that the bombardment had not cut the barbed wire were ignored by senior officers. Pilots of the Royal Flying Corps flew over the battlefield and stated that the results of the bombardment were devastating. Neither smoke nor poison gas was thought necessary to cover the attack. The troops, who were recently recruited volunteers, were considered too inexperienced to cope with tactics more complicated than a frontal advance. Faulty reconnaissance and over-optimism took a terrible toll.

The attack was not a universal failure. Several positions were captured, including Montauban, Mametz, and Grandcourt—all in the southern sector of the battlefield. But news from the northern sector was bleak.

beneath the German front lines. British spirits were high—how could anyone survive such a pounding? But the devastation was more apparent than real.

Most of the artillery shells caused minimal damage. They were insufficiently powerful to penetrate the concrete shelters of the Germans, and did little more than churn up the mud of no-man's-land, scarcely even cutting the barbed

GRINDING ON

The shock of the losses of the first day did not dissuade Haig from continuing the advance, but lessons were quickly learned. General Sir Henry Rawlinson sent his troops forward at night, followed with a brief bombardment, and then launched an attack at dawn. By July 14, the German second line was broken along Bazentin Ridge. Cavalry was used to exploit the gap. The fighting became bitter. British soldiers captured German positions, such as Delville Woods, only to face massive German counterattacks that retook the same pieces of land. Australian and New Zealand troops broke into Pozières village, gaining only one mile of ground after suffering 23,000 casualties. The Germans suffered just as badly in their counterattacks.

The intended swift war of maneuver became a lengthy combat of attrition. Haig needed a miracle weapon to break the stalemate. He

OVER THE TOP

In a war fought in trenches, the most terrifying moment for any soldier was when he was ordered to go "over the top:" to climb out of his trench and advance across no-man's-land toward the enemy defenses. Private Fred Ball, a volunteer in the Liverpool Pals, recalls such a moment during the Battle of the Somme on July 27, 1916, near Fricourt:

> Suddenly the noise of the guns eased off. For a second or two there was quiet. Then the fury of our barrage dropped like a wall of roaring sound before us. By some means the signal to advance was given and understood and we found ourselves walking forward into the mist, feeling utterly naked. Who can express the sensations of men brought up in trench warfare suddenly divested of every scrap of shelter? Forward we stumbled into a mist that seemed to grow ever thicker .... All at once I became conscious of another sound. A noise like the crisp crackle of twigs and branches, burning in a bonfire just beyond my vision in the mist, made me think I must be approaching some burning building. I realised, when my neighbour on the right dropped with a bullet in the abdomen, that the noise was machine-gun and rifle-fire, and I felt the tiniest bit happier when I touched my entrenching tool which, contrary to regulations, was attached to the front of my equipment [like armor] instead of the side.

Quoted in EVERYMAN AT WAR *(published in 1930; republished by Robinson in 1997).*

A new recruit in the British Army during World War I. This young private of the Devonshire Regiment displays the smart appearance of the typical Tommy before he arrived on the Western Front. Privates were known as Tommies after the fictitious Thomas Atkins, whose name was used on sample recruiting forms.

thought he had it in the form of a device undetected by the Germans: the tank. Haig had wanted this tracked armored gun platform ready by July 1, but manufacture was delayed and only 32 were ready by September. On September 15, they lumbered into action. Many of them simply broke down, but the few that pushed on across the mud of the battlefield were impressive and helped the soldiers gain their objectives. At Thiepval, three tanks were sufficient to terrify the Germans into abandoning the village to the British.

On November 13, the last two German defenses on the Somme battlefield fell, at Beaumont-Hamel and Beaucourt. The struggle was finally over. It had cost the British 420,000 casualties, the French 205,000, and the Germans approximately 680,000. It seemed to mark the culmination of the war, and many thought it was a time for making peace. War optimism in Britain was devastated and never really recovered. Entire groups of young men who had volunteered to fight together—the "pals regiments"—had been wiped out, and this caused tremendous grief in towns and villages across England.

Strategically, the Allies had advanced five miles. It was much too costly a victory; from this point onward, the British Army put greater effort into improving its battlefield tactics.

Below, *A dead German soldier* *in a trench at Beaumont-Hamel. Beaumont-Hamel was one of the last German defenses to be captured by Allied soldiers during the Somme offensive.*

BEAUMONT-HAMEL

Allied troops shelter in a dugout
during a lull in the fighting.
World War I became dominated by
trench warfare, as the conflict turned
into a long war of attrition. Life in the
trenches was experienced by
practically every soldier, officers and
privates alike.

IGHTING BEGAN at Beaumont-Hamel at 7:20 A.M. with a massive explosion on Hawthorn Ridge. The British artillery barrage ceased, and two platoons of the 29th Division dashed forward to capture the crater. But the Germans were far from stunned, and had taken up positions on the far side of the crater, and directed their fire at the Fusiliers.

Rather than being a shock start to the day's fighting, the mine explosion had alerted the Germans to an attack, and contributed to the high number of British casualties. Waves of British troops climbed out of their trenches to walk into the fire of German rifles, mortars, machine guns, and artillery.

The first British wave faltered and fell back to the trenches. At 9:15 A.M., the 1st Newfoundland Regiment was ordered forward. It was a massacre. All officers and more than 700 infantry fell.

The 4th Division fared little better in the Beaumont-Hamel area. Some of their soldiers entered the German lines, but the failure of other divisions on either side of them left them stranded—some to be captured, some to drift back. German counterattacks forced the British back. All in all, VIII Corps (containing the 4th and 29th Divisions) suffered 14,000 casualties—more than any other corps during the Battle of the Somme.

PLAN OF BATTLE

The Battle of the Somme might more accurately be named for the River Ancre, which bisects the battlefield. The British Fourth Army positions stretched from Gommecourt in the north to Maricourt in the south, with the Somme running along the southern flank. The Germans held the high ground, and it was this that the British attempted to capture on the first day. The battle continued for several weeks after the first dreadful day. The French advanced on either side of the River Somme. The British eventually pushed the Germans off the ridges, despite heavy counterattacks—and at great cost to both sides. In all, a 20-mile-long (32-km) by 7-mile-wide (11.5 km) strip of land stretching from Beaumont-Hamel to Chaulnes was gained by the Allied forces.

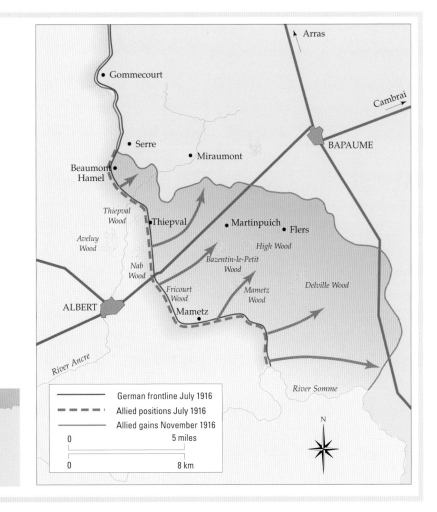

———	German frontline July 1916
– – – –	Allied positions July 1916
———	Allied gains November 1916

0 — 5 miles
0 — 8 km

BEAUMONT-HAMEL

THE BEAUMONT-HAMEL NEWFOUNDLAND MEMORIAL PARK, at the center of the Somme battlefield, is one of the best preserved areas of trenches on the Western Front. The land was bought by the Government of Newfoundland after the war, and the park was opened in 1925 by Earl Haig. The park represents in microcosm the conditions faced by many soldiers on that terrible day of July 1, 1916.

Left, *The 51st (Highland) Division Monument (8)* *stands on the German front line, which the 51st Division captured on 13 November, 1916.*

Above, *Hawthorn Ridge Cemetery (11)* *stands beside the Hawthorn Ridge Crater, the result of a massive mine explosion only minutes before the start of the battle on the morning of July 1, 1916.*

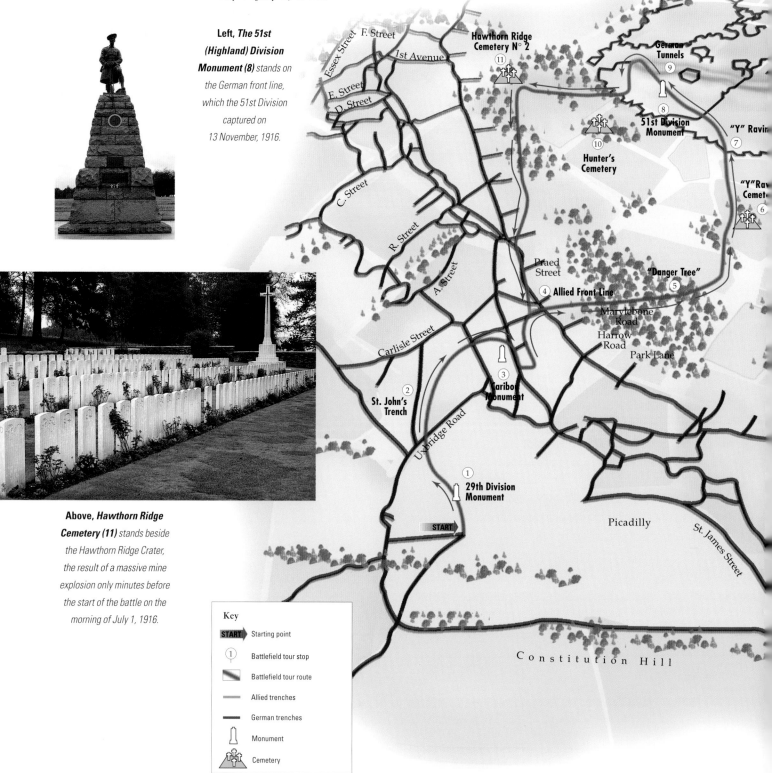

Essex Street F. Street
1st Avenue
E. Street
D. Street
C. Street
R. Street
A. Street
Carlisle Street

Hawthorn Ridge Cemetery N° 2 (11)

German Tunnels (9)

51st Division Monument (8)

"Y" Ravine (7)

Hunter's Cemetery (10)

"Y" Ravine Cemetery (6)

Praed Street

"Danger Tree" (5)

(4) Allied Front Line

Marylebone Road

Harrow Road

Park Lane

Caribou Monument (3)

(2)

St. John's Trench

Uxbridge Road

(1) 29th Division Monument

START

Picadilly

St. James Street

Constitution Hill

Key

START — Starting point

① — Battlefield tour stop

— Battlefield tour route

— Allied trenches

— German trenches

— Monument

— Cemetery

Above, *A rusting gun carriage,* half-buried and almost hidden by greenery, is a stark reminder of the intensity of fighting that this land was witness to in 1916.

GETTING THERE

LOCATION: *Northern France, south of Arras.*

VISITOR INFORMATION: *Albert Tourist Information Center, 9 Rue Jambetta, Albert, 80300 France.*

TELEPHONE: *03-22-751-642*

DIRECTIONS: *9 miles (14.5 km) north of Albert. Take D6 to Gommecourt, then D919 to Serre.*

TOUR DISTANCE: *1 mile (1.5 km).*

Above, *Hunter's Cemetery* (10) *is a circular cemetery for 46 Highlanders who were buried in a shell crater soon after the November attack. It possibly takes its name from the company commander whose men buried the dead.*

Above, *When walking around the trenches,* *the visitor should try to imagine the park without trees and the grass as mud, for that was how the battlefield looked in 1916.*

Left, *At the highest point* *of the Beaumont-Hamel Newfoundland Memorial Park is a large bronze caribou (3)—the 1st Newfoundland Regiment's emblem. At the monument's base are the names of 814 members of the regiment who have no known grave.*

Shaftesbury Avenue

Charing Cross

New Trench

Regent Street

Long

Acre

N

THE MUD OF FLANDERS

Above, ***British troops*** *in hastily dug trenches await the signal to resume the attack during the Battle of Ypres. Their helmets are spattered with crudely applied camouflage.*

Left, *The Cloth Hall at Ypres.* *An outstanding example of medieval architecture, it was completely destroyed during World War I, but was later rebuilt in the exact image of the original. It now houses a major museum to the war in Flanders.*

BACKGROUND TO BATTLE

In April 1917, the French launched a massive assault on the German lines north of Reims in northeast France, the Nivelle offensive—it was a disaster. Over 130,000 Frenchmen were casualties in the first five days, and little territory was gained. The strain on the French Army was too much, and mutinies broke out.

France was now on the edge of defeat; it was left to the British to carry the attack forward. British commander, General Sir Douglas Haig looked north to Belgium and planned his offensive.

On the morning of June 7, 1917, massive mines exploded beneath Messines Ridge with such devastating effect that the noise was heard in London. Those German defenders who were neither vaporized nor buried by the blast were so stunned that they were taken as prisoners without resistance. The British quickly captured the ridge, and the Germans considered evacuating part of Belgium.

The victory gave Haig the confidence he needed to plan a major offensive just east of the town of Ypres.

NEVER HAS THE LANDSCAPE OF WAR been more important than during the British offensive known as the Third Battle of Ypres (also called Passchendaele) in 1917. In this part of northwestern Belgium, the soil is clay. Rain cannot pass through the fine-grained, silicate-rich material, rather it settles in pools on the surface, making a quagmire for soldiers. Geologists were employed by the British army to analyze the land and suggest suitable tactics. Their advice, not surprisingly, was to attack when conditions were likely to be driest. Weather records from the previous 80 years indicated that August should offer three weeks without rain. As it happened, the rain came early in 1917, and didn't let up. Even today, farmers periodically uncover the remains of missing soldiers who drowned in the mud of Flanders.

PASSCHENDAELE RIDGE

Seven miles east of the town of Ypres lies a ridge of high ground containing the village of Passchendaele. This was the target for the Allied forces on the front line just outside Ypres. In preparation for the assault, 3,000 artillery guns pounded the German defenses; four-and-three-quarter tons of shells landed on each yard of their front line. One result was the destruction of the region's drainage system, which had evolved over hundreds of years; canals were shattered and channels filled in. Above the battlefield raged intense aerial combat in which the Royal Flying Corps gained a tenuous supremacy over German aircraft. The infantry assault began on July 31, at 3.50 A.M., in heavy mist.

The initial attack went well. The ridges of Bixschoote, Pilckem, and St. Julien were all captured. If the momentum continued, every objective would soon lie in Allied hands. Then it began to rain. The rain became a torrent that lasted two weeks. The land turned into a swamp, and the attack was bogged down. The

Above, *Battlefield in Passchendaele* in the fall of 1917, showing the sea of mud and craters faced by British soldiers. A wrecked British tank has been abandoned.

Below, *A wreath of poppies* laid at the grave of an unidentified Australian soldier who died during the Battle of Ypres.

Left, *A British Mark IV tank* that was deployed in the Battle of Ypres to exploit weakness in the enemy lines. Despite their imporsing demeanor, the tanks frequently became bogged down in the mud and were rendered useless.

Germans used the pause in the fighting to reinforce their positions. The attack resumed on August 16, and the allies captured Langemark. Then rain set in again. Soldiers stood knee-deep in mud.

BRIDGING THE MORASS

British commander, General Sir Douglas Haig now canceled the attack and began constructing roads across the muddy swamp. Using wooden planks and logs, engineers built roads at night, but the Germans knew what they were

LUCKY ESCAPE

In the first two weeks of August 1917, rain set in on the Ypres battlefield and transformed it into a quagmire, where animals and soldiers had to watch their step or vanish into mud-filled craters. Rifleman Winterbourne describes his experience with the mud of Flanders:

We got up and moved on, over this broken-up Jargon Trench and on up the slope. Beyond the trench it was soft going, but it seemed to be perfectly good ground—as good as any ground was around there at that time. All of a sudden I put one foot down and the next moment I was through the earth and in a bog up to my armpits. Well, our blokes were moving on so fast they didn't see what had happened. I was there absolutely on my own and sinking deeper and deeper, because the more I struggled, trying to get one leg up to get myself out, the deeper I went in. Fortunately the next wave came up and two runners of the 2nd London Fusiliers saw me and stopped. They got on either side and held out their rifles and that gave me some purchase to get out. There was no good shouting for help because there was so much racket going on and shells bursting all around that no one would have heard you. But I was lucky. My goodness, I was lucky!

Quoted in THEY CALLED IT PASSCHENDAELE *by Lyn Macdonald (Michael Joseph, 1978).*

A British soldier on lookout duty in a trench. The offensive at Ypres was designed to break the stalemate of trench warfare on the Western Front. (Tinted contemporary postcard.)

attempting and shelled them remorselessly. Roads were destroyed and rebuilt over and over again. Despite the endless rain, water had to be brought up to the front line because the pools surrounding the men were contaminated by decaying bodies and poison gas shells. The battlefield was apocalyptic. Every tree had been blown to splinters; all that remained was a sea of mud punctured by shell craters.

The battle resumed on September 20, and British and Australian soldiers streamed forward. In a fierce counterattack the Germans used mustard gas for the first time in the war. The Allies edged toward Polygon Wood and Gheluvelt in the south and Zonnebeke in the middle of the battlefield. On September 26, the Australians had the bizarre experience of advancing across Gheluvelt plateau in a dust storm caused by dried mud being thrown into the air by artillery shells. In October there was more rain, but the assault continued and Passchendaele village was within the grasp of the Allies. To reach it, the soldiers needed to march across two-and-a-half miles of wooden tracks.

On November 6, Canadian soldiers finally entered Passchendaele and pushed the Germans over the other side of the ridge. The battle was won—but at an enormous cost. There were 300,000 casualties among the Allied forces. Of these, 40,000 were never found—the mud had swallowed them up. The Germans lost 260,000 soldiers. The battle was termed an Allied victory, but Belgium still lay in German hands, and the Germans would return with a ferocious new offensive early the following year.

YPRES

To the east of Ypres, within a half-mile (1 km) of the farthest point reached in Belgium by British forces during World War I, lies the British Military Cemetery of Tyne Cot. It contains the largest number of men buried in any Commonwealth war cemetery, and is a moving memorial to the sacrifice of British soldiers in the war against Germany. The graves are spartan, but relatives leave messages at the base of the graves, along with single poppies.

The idea of creating such a monumental place of commemoration was born out of the horror and sadness everyone felt at the unprecedented losses on the Western Front. The Imperial War Graves Commission was incorporated by Royal Charter in 1917, and the duties formally laid upon it were the permanent marking and care of the graves of the fallen, and the commemoration by name of those who had no known grave.

The Commission aimed from the beginning to create memorials that reflected the equal sacrifice of all who fought and died, and so no individual soldier was to be marked out or given a bigger monument. All headstones were to be identically simple in design, standing 2 foot 8 inches (813 mm) high, with the badge of the service or regiment engraved at the top, and below it the rank, name, unit, date of death, and age of the soldier; beneath that is inscribed a cross or other religious emblem; and at the base, if desired, is an inscription chosen by the family.

Today, there are Commonwealth cemeteries all over the world, and each is perfectly maintained by a small army of gardeners. In France and Belgium, these are often people who served in the British forces and now live nearby, and it is their work that is crucial to creating the spirit of peace and contemplation that these cemeteries inspire.

PLAN OF BATTLE

The Third Battle of Ypres began on July 31, 1917 and lasted over three months. The British 5th Army, commanded by General Hubert de la Poer Gough, bore the brunt of the fighting. One corps of the 2nd Army (under Lieutenant General Herbert Charles Onslow Plumer) stood on its right flank, and the French 1st army (under General Francois Anthoine) stood on its left flank. Opposing them was the German 4th Army, commanded by General Armin. The British army included Canadians, Australians, and New Zealanders. Its objective was the ridges of high ground to the east, held by the Germans, with the village of Passchendaele at their center.

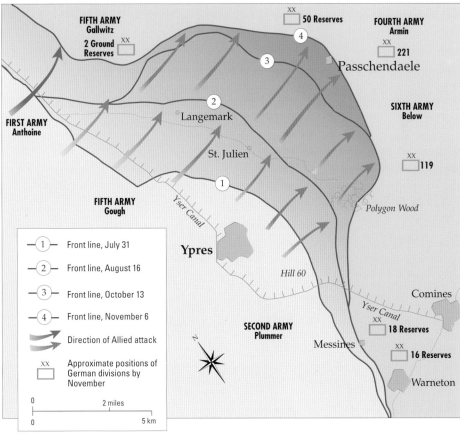

- ①— Front line, July 31
- ②— Front line, August 16
- ③— Front line, October 13
- ④— Front line, November 6
- → Direction of Allied attack
- ⬚ xx Approximate positions of German divisions by November

0   2 miles

0   5 km

YPRES

T HE BELGIAN TOWN OF YPRES (IEPER) was a jewel of medieval architecture before it was completely destroyed by German artillery. After World War I, it was painstakingly reconstructed, and today it is again a beautiful town to visit as the starting point for a driving tour of the villages around which the Third Battle of Ypres focused.

Right, *The Menin Gate (14)* *in Ypres is one of the most visited memorials of World War I. Built on the gateway through which many soldiers passed on their way to battle, it commemorates 54,896 British and Commonwealth soldiers who were lost without trace. Every evening at 8:00 P.M. the "Last Post" is played beneath the arch by members of the local fire department.*

Below, *The small Flemish market town of Ypres (1)* *was a scene of fighting for all four years of World War I. The British Front line in the area projected into German-held territory, making Ypres an important salient on the Western Front.*

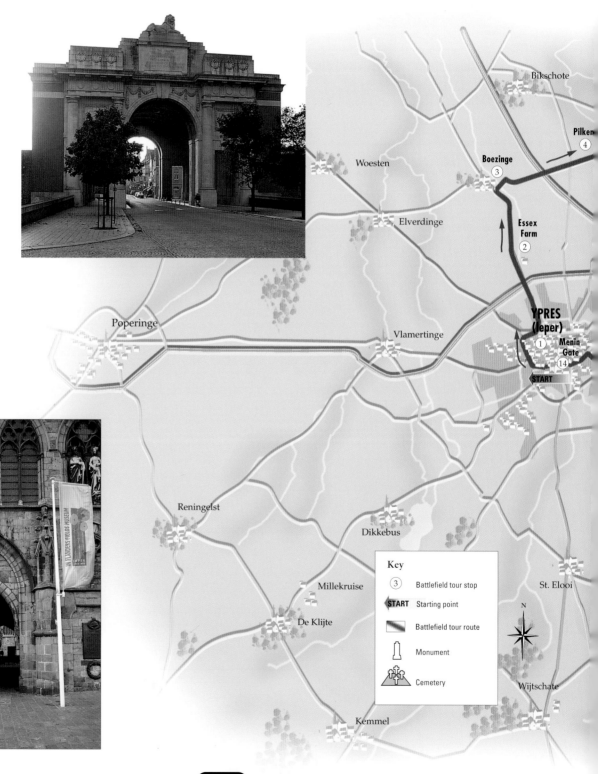

Left, *Langemark (5)* extends for a mile along was captured by the Allies on August 16. There is an important German military cemetery here, and concrete blockhouses used by the Germans.

PILCKEM

Pilckem (4) was one of the first objectives captured by the British. The largest German bunker still standing in this area can be seen near the Pilckem Road.

ST. JULIEN

St. Julien (7) was captured on August 3. Nearby, at Vancouver Corner, is the Canadian Memorial (6)—a pillar surmounted by the bust of a soldier, commemorating the deaths of 2,000 Canadians.

PASSCHENDAELE (PASSENDALE)

The village of Passchendaele (8) was the final objective of the great Ypres offensive, and was captured on November 6.

ZONNEBEKE

Zonnebeke (10) was completely destroyed in the battle—reduced to a sea of mud. Nearby is a clay quarry in which a preserved dugout was recently uncovered.

POLYGON WOOD

Polygon Wood (11) was the scene of fierce fighting between Australians and Germans. The cemetery here contains New Zealand and Australian memorials.

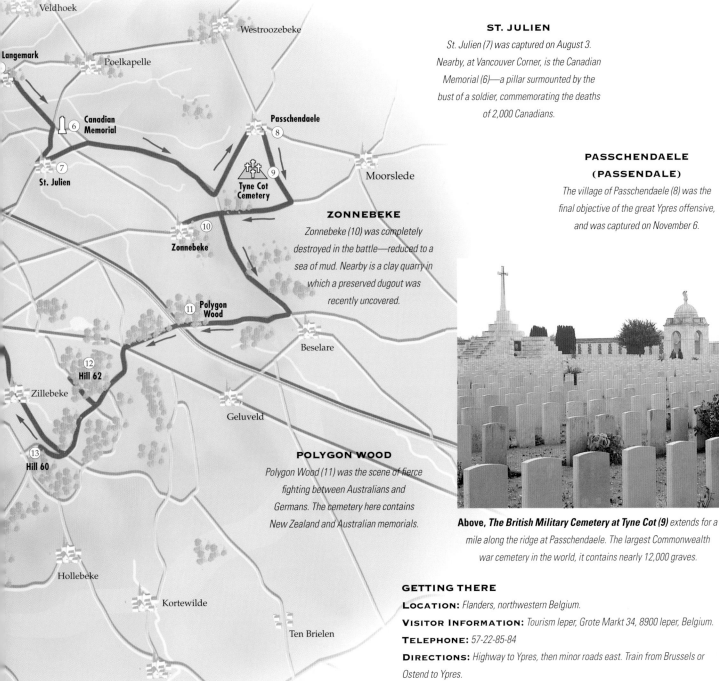

Above, *The British Military Cemetery at Tyne Cot (9)* extends for a mile along the ridge at Passchendaele. The largest Commonwealth war cemetery in the world, it contains nearly 12,000 graves.

GETTING THERE

LOCATION: *Flanders, northwestern Belgium.*

VISITOR INFORMATION: *Tourism Ieper, Grote Markt 34, 8900 Ieper, Belgium.*

TELEPHONE: *57-22-85-84*

DIRECTIONS: *Highway to Ypres, then minor roads east. Train from Brussels or Ostend to Ypres.*

TOUR DISTANCE: *23 miles (37 km).*

INVADING NAZI EUROPE

Above, *General Dwight D. Eisenhower,* Supreme Commander of the Allied forces on D day, talks to soldiers of the U.S. 82nd Airborne Division just before they leave to be dropped behind German lines on the morning of June 6, 1944.

Left, *Gold beach at Arromanches* was once home to a Mulberry harbour, the remains of which are still visible. This artificial breakwater was made in section in Great Britain, towed across the Channel, and sunk into place after D Day, providing a safe port from which war supplies could be discharged to the Allied troops.

JUNE 6, 1944 has been called the most important day in the twentieth century. It was on that date that Allied forces landed in Nazi-occupied France and challenged Adolf Hitler's control of western Europe. It was an awesome undertaking. As one British supply officer involved in the preparations described it: "Something comparable to the city of Birmingham [second largest city in the United Kingdom] hasn't merely got to be shifted: it's got to be kept moving when it's on the other side ... we must take everything with us, and take it in the teeth of the fiercest opposition." To enter France, the Allies faced a formidable line of defense along the Atlantic coast.

THE ATLANTIC WALL

The Atlantic Wall stretched over 1,615 miles (2,600 km) from the Arctic Circle to the Spanish border. From 1940 onward, the Germans built massive concrete bunkers along the French coast—first to prepare for an invasion of Britain, then to control the approach of an invading Allied fleet. Many of the concrete gun emplacements still stand on the coast. In just one month during 1943, about 995,000 cubic yards (760,000 cubic meters) of concrete was poured into the construction of the Atlantic Wall,

BACKGROUND TO BATTLE

The turning point of World War II occurred in 1943, when the previously victorious German Army was stopped by the Russians in two major battles— at Stalingrad and Kursk.

At about the same time, Allied forces landed in Italy. Hitler faced assaults on two fronts, and this fatally divided his forces.

Between May 15 and May 25, 1943, British Prime Minister Winston Churchill and U.S. President Franklin D. Roosevelt met at the Trident conference in Washington. They agreed on two main points: to continue the massive bomb offensive against Germany, and to launch a cross-Channel invasion of Europe— Operation Overlord.

Planning began immediately, and May, 1944 was selected as the time of attack. The number of U.S. forces in Britain was greatly increased, and intensive training began.

A campaign of deception, code-named Operation Bodyguard, was launched to confuse German intelligence. It worked so well that, all the way up until D Day, Hitler and his staff expected the main attack to come in the Pas de Calais region farther north, and therefore delayed reinforcements to Normandy.

Left, *The Batterie de Longues. This formidable German artillery battery was one of many gun emplacements built along the coast of northern France as part of Hitler's Atlantic Wall defenses, but is the only one to still have its guns. These weapons gave the Allied ships a pounding on the morning of June 6, 1944.*

and the average continued to be about 261,000 cubic yards (200,000 cubic meters) per month until April 1944. In 1943, Field Marshal Erwin Rommel took command of the defenses and increased the emphasis on stopping an invasion force on the beaches, prior to a German counterattack. More than six million mines were laid on the beaches. Many of these were raised out of the sand on wooden posts in order to sink boats. There were also thousands of obstacles known as hedgehogs—steel spikes intended to impede the progress of enemy tanks.

In the face of this came an armada of 4,000 Allied ships, bearing 176,000 men. The area chosen for the invasion was the beaches east of the Cotentin Peninsula in Normandy. Five landing points were identified and were codenamed Utah, Omaha, Gold, Juno, and Sword. United

HITTING THE BEACH

The Allied bombardment of the Normandy beaches raised the confidence of the troops who were about to land, but when their landing craft opened, they were shocked by the ferocity of the German fire directed at them. U.S. Sergeant John Slaughter of the 29th Infantry Division, then aged just 19, describes the scene at Omaha beach:

As my turn came to exit [the landing craft], I sat on the edge of the bucking ramp trying to time my leap on the down cycle. I sat there too long, causing a bottleneck and endangering myself as well as the men that followed. The one-inch steel ramp was going up and down in the surf, rising as much as six or seven feet; I was afraid it would slam me on the head. One of the men was hit and died instantly.... There were dead men floating in the water and there were live men acting dead, letting the tide take them in. I was crouched down to chin-deep in the water when I saw mortar shells zeroing in at the water's edge. Sand began to kick up from small arms fire from the bluffs. It became apparent that it was past time to get the hell across that beach. I don't know how long we were in the water before the move was made, but I guess close to an hour.

Quoted in NOTHING LESS THAN VICTORY *by Russell Miller (Michael Joseph, 1993).*

U.S. troops in landing craft *head for Omaha beach on the morning of June 6, 1944.*

States General Dwight D. Eisenhower was appointed Supreme Commander, and British General Bernard Law Montgomery was in command of ground forces. The U.S. 1st Army, under Lieutenant General Omar N. Bradley, was to land at Utah and Omaha. The British 2nd Army, under General Dempsey, with a Canadian corps, was to land at Gold, Juno, and Sword. A million Allied soldiers were poised to invade the Continent. June 5 was selected as D Day, but because of a poor weather forecast, the operation was postponed. The Allied meteorological staff announced "relatively good weather" for June 6—the invasion was on.

BLOODY OMAHA

Paratroopers dropped behind enemy lines, and a massive bombardment was delivered by Allied aircraft and ships as the landing craft streamed toward the beaches. At Omaha, the Allied preparation appeared largely ineffective. The aircraft dropped most of their bombs behind the German fortifications for fear of striking Allied ships, and other bombs bounced off the tough concrete bunkers. The sea was rough, and many of the amphibious tanks were swamped by waves—they sank to the bottom, with their crews trapped inside. Only six of the 33 tanks sent ashore reached the beach. Many U.S. soldiers drowned in the approach. When the survivors reached the shore, they were met by a storm of fire, as the German artillery aimed straight down onto the beach. Most of the troops left their packs and heavy weapons on the landing boats, rather than risk taking them into the rough water;

Below, "Under New Management": *Hindenburg Bastion, part of Hitler's formidable Atlantic Wall defenses, captured by British troops on D Day.*

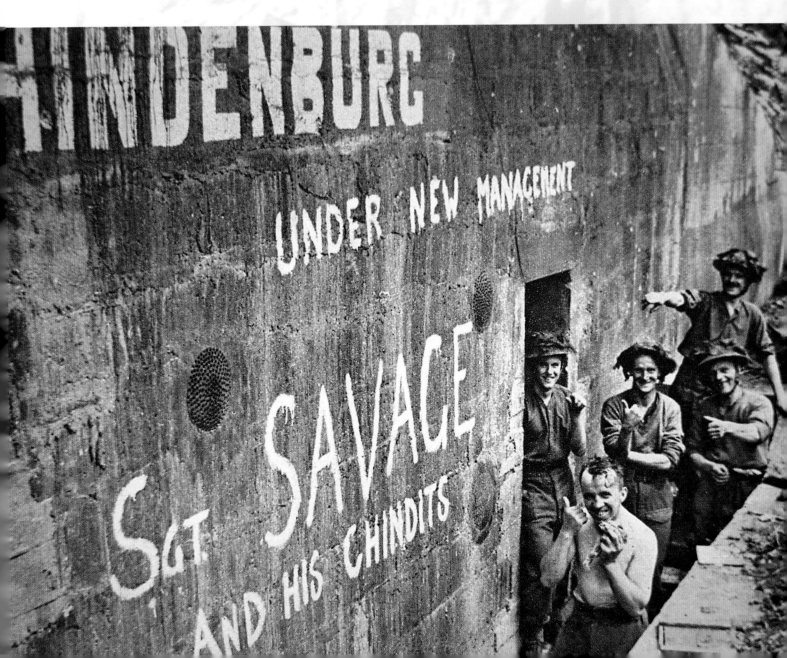

without machine guns or flamethrowers, they had only pistols and rifles. Bodies lay thick on the beach, and soldiers crouched for cover beneath the sea wall.

On Gold, the British had similar problems. Rough seas and strong defenses hampered their landing, but their specially designed tanks, with flails for exploding mines, gave some assistance. The British managed to press ahead, minus 1,000 casualties. On Juno, seasick Canadians stumbled ashore to be greeted by a mass of exploded bodies and equipment. But the Canadians were bent on revenge for a previously failed landing at Dieppe, and by the end of the day they had advanced farther inland than any of the other Allied forces. They too suffered 1,000 casualties. Sword claimed another 1,000 soldiers, but the troops there managed to break the German defenses and advance a little way. On Utah, a mistake involving the intended landing area saved U.S. soldiers from the more heavily defended section of the beach, and they also moved inland. On bloody Omaha, however, the U.S. forces lost 3,000 men by nightfall.

D Day was a success—but at a terrible cost. Over the following days, increasing numbers of men and supplies were landed on the beaches, but the initial landings were a foretaste of the struggle that lay ahead as the Allies fought to break out of Normandy.

NORMANDY

Above, _A rare photograph taken during the landing at Omaha_
beach, _showing troops taking cover on the shingle against_
devastating German fire.

Memorials and the remains of tanks and bunkers dot the Normandy coast. One of the most dramatic monuments is at Pointe du Hoc, overlooking Omaha beach. Here, a stone obelisk commemorating a daring raid by U.S. Rangers stands on the remains of a German bunker.

The destruction of German gun batteries identified in the bunkers that guarded this stretch of the coast was a top priority, and the awesome task of scaling the cliffs to knock out the gun batteries was given to the U.S. 2nd Ranger Battalion. At 4:15 A.M. on D Day, the Rangers approached the cliffs. The situation did not look good. Two of their craft had been blown up by German guns, and they were moving toward the wrong landing point. Their landing craft came under heavy fire as the Rangers approached the beach. They fired rocket lines at the cliffs, but the heavy, wet ropes reached no farther than 50 feet (15 meters).

With only ladders and daggers to help them, the Rangers tackled the 100-foot (30-meter) face of the cliff, with rifle and machine-gun fire all around them. After 30 minutes, 100 Rangers had scaled the cliffs. They moved forward to destroy their target—but there were no guns! Allied intelligence had got it wrong.

The troops patrolled until they eventually located—and destroyed—the guns that were destined for the bunkers. German soldiers counterattacked, however, and a fierce two-day battle ensued until the Rangers were eventually relieved.

PLAN OF BATTLE

Allied forces landed to the east of the Cotentin Peninsula, between Cherbourg and Caen. 176,000 troops attacked on five beaches, code-named Utah, Omaha, Gold, Juno, and Sword. They were opposed by the German 7th Army, which was made up of veteran German soldiers and less effective Axis allies.

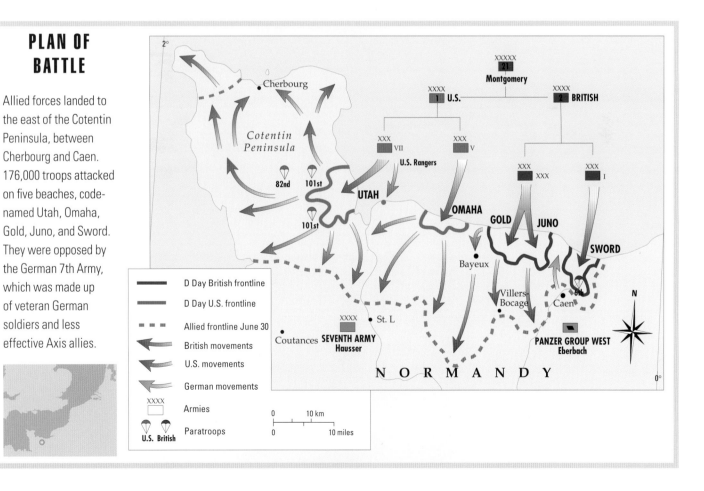

NORMANDY

On June 6, 1944, Omaha beach was hell on earth. Today, it is four miles of sand in the shape of a crescent moon, lapped by a shallow tide—a favorite vacation resort. There are numerous memorials and the remains of tanks and bunkers along the entire Normandy coast from Cherbourg to Caen.

Below, **_The American National Cemetery_** and memorial at St. Laurent (6) contains over 9,000 graves. A flag-lowering ceremony takes place every evening, just before 6:00 P.M.

POINTE DU HOC

A gun battery captured by U.S. Rangers at Omaha is on display at Pointe du Hoc (8), where there is a Rangers Museum and the remains of bunkers. The ground nearby is scarred with huge craters left by the Allied aerial and naval bombardment prior to D Day.

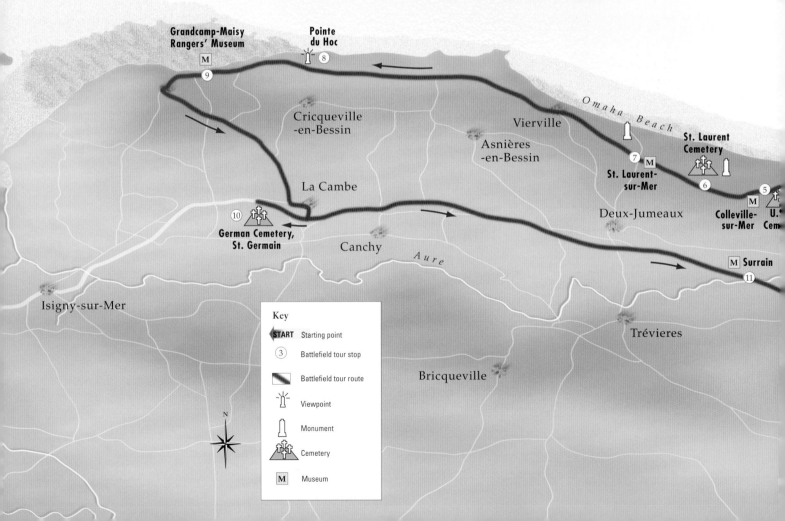

Grandcamp-Maisy
Rangers' Museum

Pointe
du Hoc
⑧

M
⑨

Cricqueville
-en-Bessin

Omaha Beach

Vierville

St. Laurent
Cemetery

Asnières
-en-Bessin

⑦ M

St. Laurent-
sur-Mer

⑥

La Cambe

⑤

Colleville-
sur-Mer

U.
Cem

M

Deux-Jumeaux

⑩

German Cemetery,
St. Germain

Canchy

Aure

M Surrain

⑪

Isigny-sur-Mer

Trévieres

Bricqueville

Key

START Starting point

③ Battlefield tour stop

  Battlefield tour route

  Viewpoint

  Monument

  Cemetery

M Museum

GETTING THERE

LOCATION: *Normandy, northern France.*

VISITOR INFORMATION: *Office du Tourisme, B.P. 343, 14403 Bayeux, France.*

TELEPHONE: *02 31 51 28 28*

DIRECTIONS: *From Bayeux, take D6 north to Port-en-Bessin, and then the D514 east along the coast that formed Omaha beach, stopping for walks and museums at Colleville-sur-Mer, St-Laurent-sur-Mer, Pointe du Hoc, and Grandcamp-Maisy.*

TOUR DISTANCE: *51 miles (82.5 km).*

Below, *The Omaha Museum*
is guarded by a U.S. Sherman
tank and a 155 mm cannon.

BAYEUX

Bayeux (1) was the first French town to be liberated. Its commemorations include the Battle of Normandy Museum and a British war memorial.

ARROMANCHES: GOLD BEACH

The remains of the concrete movable Mulberry Harbour, designed to provide a secure landing for the troops, mark the site of Gold beach at Arromanches (5).

DEATH IN THE ARDENNES

Above, *Heavily loaded U.S. Army trucks* often got bogged down in mud—
victims of the wet winter weather of the Ardennes.

Left, *The Liberty Milestone* in Bastogne is the last of a series of milestones from
Normandy to Bastogne marking the route of General Patton's 3rd Army as they
helped to liberate France and Belgium.

THE DENSE AND ANCIENT FOREST of the Ardennes lies on the border between Belgium and Germany. Picturesque little villages are scattered among the trees. Wild boar can still be hunted here, and the region is famous for its rich, coarse pâté. In December 1944, its inhabitants were settling in for a typical Ardennes winter. Heavy fog swirled among the trees and dampness clung to the roads, thickening some of them with mud. A light snow began to fall, and the Belgians were certain they would have a white Christmas. Their mood was optimistic after four years of Nazi occupation, because they knew that the Allies were advancing on all fronts, liberating town after town in Europe. Soon the German war machine would collapse, and the Belgians could look forward to the sweetest Christmas present of all—freedom. But their optimism was premature. Hitler had a final surprise in store.

CLOAKED IN FOG

On December 16, the silence of the Ardennes forest was broken by the rumble of three S.S. Panzer armies. Although the Germans were in retreat elsewhere, Hitler had gathered some of his best troops and strongest tank formations to lead a counterattack that aimed to stop the Western Allies in their tracks. Through the morning mist came veteran German assault troops, accompanied by some of their most frightening tanks, including the awesome Tiger.

BACKGROUND TO BATTLE

By December 1944, World War II should have been over in Europe. Germany was under attack by two massive forces. The Allies had landed successfully at Normandy and were advancing steadily toward the Rhine, while the Soviet Army was steamrolling across eastern Europe toward Berlin.

Hitler, the supreme German military commander, could not fight a war on two fronts. He had to make a deal with one of his adversaries. If he could detach one enemy from the war, he could pitch all of his forces against the other.

Hitler knew that a deal with Russia was impossible; German forces had wreaked appalling destruction on the country and its people. He therefore looked west to the Allies, in the hope of striking a deal that would save Germany from total defeat and leave some of the Third Reich intact.

To achieve this, Hitler had to show the Allies that the Germans retained enough strength to make the continued advance to the Rhine too costly for either side to contemplate. This was the reasoning behind the German offensive in the Ardennes. It was Hitler's last gamble.

Up until this point, the 80-mile (128-km) long Ardennes sector had been thinly held by U.S. soldiers. The Americans were taken completely by surprise. The skies over the Ardennes were overcast, which severely limited Allied air activity and support. The Belgian landscape was shrouded in fog, and visibility was restricted to less than 100 yards. This favored German weapons, such as machine pistols, whereas American riflemen had little opportunity to put their marksmanship to the test. Thick mud bogged down Allied trucks, and the arrival of snow increased the difficulty of shifting troops and supplies around the battlefield. A spearhead of English-speaking Germans in American uniforms compounded the confusion.

The U.S. 28th and 106th Divisions collapsed before the onslaught. To the north, U.S. V Corps held firm, as did the U.S. 4th Division in the south. In true blitzkrieg style, the German

Above, *The Battle of the Bulge* *began with the advance of German troops of S.S.-Panzergrenadier-Regiment 1.*

BAD LUCK

Success in a tank battle depended not only on the vehicles, but on the quality of the men driving them—and sometimes on sheer luck. Arndt Fischer, commanding a Panzer tank during the Battle of the Bulge, describes how difficult it was to know exactly what was happening from inside the noisy, cramped hull of a tank:

To start with I did not notice any fighting and therefore wanted to cross the bridge [over the Ambleve, near Ligneuville]. On the bend before the bridge I was shot up from behind. My Panzer went up in flames. We got out of the tank under machine gun and rifle fire coming from nearby houses. We were burning like torches, as only a couple of hours before we had re-fuelled, including our jerrycans, in Bullingen. In doing so we had soaked our clothing in petrol. My driver never managed to get out and was burned to death.

Quoted in THE DEVIL'S ADJUTANT *by Michael Reynolds (Spellmount, 1995).*

Heavily armed German S.S. troops *in front of a captured U.S. armored car.*

The chilled and exhausted face of a U.S. soldier during the Battle of the Bulge.

forces drove on between the points of resistance, toward the Meuse River, creating the bulge in Allied lines from which the battle derives its name. In response, General Dwight D. Eisenhower, the Allies' Supreme Commander, quickly committed his reserves. The U.S. 101st Airborne Division arrived in the town of Bastogne to confront the 5th Panzer Army, and the 82nd strengthened the northern flank. In the south, Lieutenant General George S. Patton, Jr., halted his 3rd Army and turned it around to attack the German southern flank.

"NUTS!"

The battle now centered on the town of Bastogne. About 18,000 U.S. soldiers were courageously holding the town against the 5th Panzer Army. Elsewhere, German tanks were

Below, *Snow-covered M4 Sherman tanks* of the U.S. 40th Tank Battalion wait to go into action near St. Vith.

grinding to a halt due to a lack of gasoline, and suffering from Allied counterattacks. Hitler now became obsessed with taking Bastogne. On December 22, German officers waved a flag of truce and delivered a note to Brigadier General Anthony McAuliffe, who was commanding the town's defense. The note demanded that McAuliffe surrender. "Aw, nuts!" he is said to have retorted, and after consultation with his staff, it was agreed that the official U.S. response should be "Nuts!" A ferocious assault on Bastogne then began. A heavy bombardment on Christmas Eve was followed by an all-out Panzer attack on the western sector of the town.

To the south of Bastogne, Patton ordered the 4th Armored Division to "Drive like hell!" In the meantime, the sky had cleared and Allied aircraft began to bomb German supply lines. The tide was turning, and by January 2, the battle for Bastogne was over. With British and U.S. forces attacking in the north and Patton making headway in the south, Hitler had to accept defeat and withdraw his shattered Panzer divisions.

Below, *The German Cemetery at Recogne* contains the graves of 6,776 German soldiers and officers who died in the Ardennes during World War II.

THE ARDENNES

THE WOODED LANDSCAPE and narrow roads of the Ardennes are uncongenial conditions for motorized columns, which is the main reason why the initial assault of the Germans was so successful. Success was also due to the leadership of Jochen Peiper, commander of the elite 1st S.S. Panzer Division. His tanks moved rapidly along the forest roads. When he encountered pockets of resistance, he went around them in the essence of blitzkrieg warfare—avoiding small conflicts that could be resolved by follow-up troops.

Above, *U.S. troops, besieged in Bastogne* *in December 1944 by the German counterattack, search snowy fields for supplies dropped by parachute from Allied aircraft.*

Peiper pushed on to Stavelot. Only 13 U.S. soldiers defended this position, but their fearless action halted the German column, giving enough time for American reinforcements to arrive. Peiper took Stavelot, but the Americans encircled him and cut his supply line, drawing 2,000 soldiers and 200 vehicles into a pocket from which they could not escape. Peiper was captured, and the spearhead of the German assault was broken. Attention now shifted to Bastogne, and the American defense of this position in the heart of the bulge.

PLAN OF BATTLE

On December 16, three German Panzer armies, consisting of 24 divisions—ten of them armored—thrust against exhausted units of the U.S. Army, creating a bulge in the Allied lines. German armored units were equipped with the latest version of the formidable Tiger tank, which had a high-velocity 88 mm gun that far outranged any tank the Allies could field. Casualties in the Battle of the Bulge were substantial. U.S. losses included 8,477 men killed, 46,170 wounded, and 20,905 prisoners or missing. British losses were 200 killed, 239 wounded, and 969 prisoners or missing. German losses were 10,749 killed, 34,439 wounded, and 32,487 prisoners or missing.

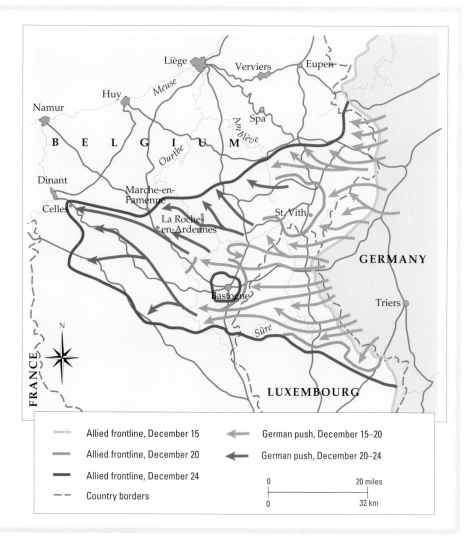

Liège
Verviers
Eupen
Huy
Meuse
Namur
Spa
B E L G I U M
Amblève
Ourthe
Dinant
Marche-en-Famenne
Celles
La Roche-en-Ardennes
St. Vith
GERMANY
Bastogne
Triers
N
Sûre
FRANCE
LUXEMBOURG

···· Allied frontline, December 15	⇐ German push, December 15–20
— Allied frontline, December 20	⇐ German push, December 20–24
— Allied frontline, December 24	0 20 miles
– – Country borders	0 32 km

ARDENNES

THE FOREST OF THE ARDENNES is a favorite vacation spot for Europeans. Camping among the lakes and trees of this surprisingly remote area in the heart of western Europe, they enjoy the good food for which the region is renowned. But located among the pretty little villages are reminders of the terrible battle fought here more than 50 years ago. A surviving Panzer tank is mounted on a concrete plinth outside a gas station. A village butcher opens to visitors his private collection of military memorabilia from the surrounding fields.

GETTING THERE

LOCATION: *The Ardennes region, eastern Belgium.*

VISITOR INFORMATION: *Royal Syndicat d'Initiative et du Tourisme Bastogne, Place McAuliffe, B-6600, Bastogne.*

TELEPHONE: *061 21 27 11*

DIRECTIONS: *By car from Brussels: take the E411 to Namur, then follow the N4 to Marche and Bastogne; from Liége: take E25 to Bastogne (exit 54); from Marche: take E40 to Bastogne.*

TOUR DISTANCE: *1½ miles (2.5 km).*

Left, *A commemorative plaque* honoring the Belgian volunteers in Patton's army, and a monument to the general himself, who came to the relief of the besieged Americans with his armored division, stands in Place Mercény (4), Bastogne .

Below, *The gun turrets of U.S. Sherman tanks* are mounted along all of the access roads to Bastogne. Boundary stones mark the perimeter of the U.S. defenses.

BASTOGNE

Rue des Kemp
Rue des Ecoles
Rue du Sablon
Rue Des Remparts
Rue des Remparts
Rue Courte
(2) McAuliffe Square
Avenue Mathieu
Ardennes Museum (3) M
Rue de Neufchâteau
Rue d'Assenois
Rue Renquin
Rue des Scieries
Patton Monument
(4) Place Mercény
Avenue Albert 1er

Above, _Mardasson Hill._ The battle for Bastogne was the climax of the fighting in the Ardennes. Mardasson Hill (1) is the site of the principal memorial to the U.S. soldiers who fought in the Battle of the Bulge. Also at Mardasson Hill is the Bastogne Historical Center, a museum of the battle, which has tanks parked outside.

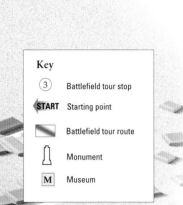

Mardasson
① U.S.A. Memorial

START

Rue Delperdange

Rue des Remparts

Place
Saint Pierre

Rue du Sablon

Rue des Jardins

Rue de la Citadelle

Rue du Vieux Moulin

Haute

Key

③   Battlefield tour stop

START   Starting point

    Battlefield tour route

    Monument

M   Museum

Right, _A bust of General McAuliffe,_ the U.S. commander of Bastogne's defense in December 1944, stands in the town's Place McAuliffe (2), named for him. A Sherman tank is also displayed here.

AFRICA, ASIA, AND OCEANIA

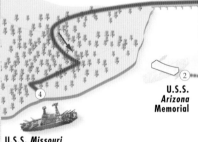

U.S.S. Arizona Memorial

U.S.S. Missouri

The clash of different peoples around the world has seen fierce battles.

In Africa and Asia, empires faltered as native armies contested the rights of others to rule them.

Western nations have endured some of their most testing battles fought in challenging landscapes, from the jungles of Vietnam to the blistering heat of Turkey and the tropical islands of Hawaii.

SHAKING THE EMPIRE

Above, *Lieutenant General Lord Chelmsford,* commander of the British forces at Isandlwana.

Left, *Clusters of whitewashed stones* commemorate the places where British soldiers fell during the fighting at Isandlwana.

NEWS OF THE BATTLE OF ISANDLWANA broke like a thunderclap over southern Africa. Both colonists and Africans fled southward from the border lands. Some boarded ships and quit the country altogether. It was too unbelievable. The mighty British Empire had been shaken to its roots by an army of Zulus armed with spears and shields.

INTO ZULULAND

On January 11, 1879, Lieutenant General Frederic Augustus Thesiger, second Baron Chelmsford, commander of the British forces, confidently led some 5,000 British soldiers and 8,200 native allies into Zululand in three separate columns. His men were well armed and supplied. The British soldiers carried Martini-Henry rifles which could fire up to 12 shots a minute. In addition, there were Gatling guns, rockets, and artillery firing case shot, which at close range had the effect of a giant shotgun. Opposing Chelmsford were 40,000 Zulu warriors, led by their king, Cetewayo. Some had rifles, but most fought with shields, knobkerries, throwing spears, and shorter stabbing spears called *ilthwa* by the Zulus and *assegais* by the whites. To have any chance of victory, the Zulus needed to get close to their

BACKGROUND TO BATTLE

In the history of southern Africa, the colonists took land from the native Africans, but there were also inter-tribal wars over territory. The Zulu tribe conquered neighboring tribes to form a considerable kingdom in southern Africa.

In the Transvaal, Boer settlers disputed territory with the Zulu king Cetewayo. At first, Britain supported the claims of the Zulus, but when the British Empire assumed control of the Transvaal, they came into direct conflict with the Zulu king. Some British politicians thought that the conflict could be put to good use.

As the mightiest empire in the world, the British wanted to prove to the people of Transvaal that they were worthy rulers by checking any Zulu threats. Moreover, other black tribes were restless, and it was felt that a strike against the most powerful black tribe in the region would serve as a warning to the others.

In December 1878, Sir Henry Bartle Frere, Governor of Cape Colony and High Commissioner for native affairs in South Africa, presented an ultimatum to the Zulu king which the British knew he could not accept. The next month, a British army advanced into Zululand.

enemy—and that involved a long run across open ground toward the British firing line.

Chelmsford planned to capture Cetewayo's capital at Ulundi in a large pincer movement. But by dividing his forces he also weakened them. Zulu warriors clashed with all three columns, testing their strength. On January 20, Chelmsford set up camp with his center column at the base of Mount Isandlwana. His scouts told him that Zulus were gathering nearby, and he decided to confront them before dawn on January 22. He left about 1,700 men in the camp, including 700 infantry of the 24th Regiment, and advanced to battle with the remainder. It was now that the scouts realized that Chelmsford had made a terrible error. An *impi* (army) of 20,000 Zulus, under the joint command of *inKhosi* (princes) Ntshingwayo, kaMahole, and Mavumengwana, had moved around Chelmsford's flank and lay hidden in the undulating countryside about five miles from Isandlwana.

*Right, **Battle of Isandlwana,** showing British redcoats of the 24th Regiment closing ranks as they bravely face the onslaught of the Zulus.*

"HORNS OF THE BEAST"

The Zulus attacked in a crescent formation, hoping to crush their enemy between the two flanking "horns of the beast." Lieutenant Colonel Henry Pulleine was in charge of the camp at Isandlwana. He received news of the Zulu advance, but was not unduly troubled because he was convinced that Chelmsford was dealing with the main threat. When he saw Zulu troops moving across the plain, Pulleine finally ordered his men to form up in front of the camp. Two guns began shelling the advance Zulu formations. Colonel Anthony B. E. Durnford and his mounted troops became aware of the danger when they made contact with the Zulu left horn. After delivering a volley, Durnford turned and retreated until he reached a dried riverbed. There he made a stand, holding

FIGHTING LIONS

Zulu warriors at Isandlwana considered their British foes to be as brave as lions, and their death carried the same high status as slaying a lion. Some of the ferocity of the hand-to-hand fighting between British and Zulu soldiers is captured in the memories of a warrior named uMhoti of the uKhandempemvu Regiment:

I then attacked a soldier whose bayonet pierced my shield and while he was trying to extract it, I stabbed him in the shoulder. He dropped his rifle and seized me round the neck and threw me on the ground under him. My eyes felt as if they were bursting, and I was almost choked when I succeeded in grasping the spear which was still sticking in his shoulder and forced it into his vitals and he rolled over, lifeless. My body was covered with sweat and quivering terribly with the choking I had received from this brave man.

Quoted in ANATOMY OF THE ZULU ARMY *by Ian Knight (Greenhill, 1995).*

A Zulu warrior *in magnificent battle array, with cowhide shield and stabbing spears.*

Right, *Cetewayo,* *who was king of the Zulus from 1873 until his death in 1884.*

the right flank of Pulleine's position. Pulleine had the camp covered, and the overextended redcoated line of 600 riflemen of the 24th, with their Martini-Henry rifles, forced the Zulus to ground—they sheltered in the hollows beyond the flat land around the camp.

The Zulus did not wait for long before moving around the position. Fearful of being outflanked, Durnford pulled his men back to the camp. Pulleine also decided to reduce his line. The bugles rang out, calling the 24th to retreat. Until this moment, although they outnumbered the British, the Zulus had been checked by the superior firepower of the enemy, and were unsure of their next move. Seeing the British fall back, the Zulus summoned their courage and rose again, charging toward the camp. Some of the British tried to form defensive squares, but, suddenly, all was lost. They were overrun. The Zulus' left horn swept around the camp. British and colonial soldiers now stood individually, defying the enemy—when their ammunition ran out, they fought on with bayonet and rifle-butt.

TO THE BITTER END

Zulu witnesses recount how one tall white soldier killed every warrior who approached him with his bayonet, until a Zulu shot him dead. A sailor—the servant of a naval officer on Chelmsford's staff—stood with his back to a wagon and cut down every warrior who confronted him, with a cutlass. Eventually, a Zulu crawled beneath the wagon and stabbed him from behind. Other soldiers stood back to back until overwhelmed. Captain Reginald Younghusband and a few troops extricated themselves from the chaos by climbing onto the

Above, *Members of the British Die-Hard group,* equipped with the uniforms and weapons of 1879, mark the 120th anniversary of the conflict on the battlefield of Isandlwana.

mountain. They held out while their bullets lasted, then charged down with bayonets to die in the fighting. Durnford and Pulleine were both killed in the struggle.

As the defense of the camp collapsed, the Queen's Colour, sheathed in a black leather case, was handed to Lieutenant Teignmouth Melvill. This was the Union Jack Flag with the regiment's numeral on it, and was a source of great pride—it should never fall into enemy hands. Melvill galloped out of the fighting toward the Buffalo river. He was joined by Lieutenant N. J. A. Coghill. Coghill was first to spur his horse into the river. Melvill followed, but the weight of the Colour unbalanced him and he fell into the torrent. The Colour disappeared beneath the water. Seeing Melvill in difficulty, Coghill turned back to help him. His horse was killed by Zulu bullets, but he managed to pull Melvill to the opposite bank. They climbed up the steep riverside and found a large rock. There they turned to face death together at the hands of the Zulus.

In the camp, every living creature was killed. In accordance with Zulu warrior tradition, the bodies of the British were stripped and mutilated so they could not seek revenge in the afterlife, an act that outraged white opinion. Over 1,200 British and colonists with their native allies were slaughtered. The Zulus also lost at least 1,000 dead, and many more were seriously wounded by bullets and bayonets.

After a day of pointless skirmishing, unaware of events at Isandlwana, Lord Chelmsford returned to his camp there at nightfall. Darkness screened the worst of the nightmare, but by dawn Chelmsford knew that his campaign was in tatters—and the British Empire had been severely tested.

ISANDLWANA

AT ISANDLWANA, if the British had held their position, they would have been safe, because the effect of their rifle and artillery fire was both terrifying and mystifying to the Zulus. The Zulus sheltered in hollows, as they had quickly learned that when the British artillerymen stood back from their cannons to fire them, they should lie low to avoid the incoming shells.

Eventually, the commanders of the Zulus began to taunt their warriors to stand up and fight. They began to advance at a walking pace, but at a distance of about 130 yards from the British line, they shouted their battlecry of "uSuthu!"—and charged. The sight was terrifying, and the British soldiers fell

Above, *Zulu warriors charge forward* in a reenactment of their forefathers' triumph at Isandlwana.

back in a panic toward the camp, with the Zulus outpacing them and breaking up their formations. Confusion overtook them, and Zulus surrounded every soldier.

A partial eclipse of the sun at 2:30 P.M. added to the gloom of the battlefield, which was already shrouded in smoke and dust. Soldiers fought blindly, lashing out at anyone close to them. The Zulus regarded the eclipse as an omen of great loss, because both sides were inflicting heavy casualties. Eventually, the overwhelming numbers of the Zulus assured victory. No one was spared, even the little drummerboys were hung up and butchered. Such tales of battlefield gore outraged the Victorian public at home.

PLAN OF BATTLE

This map shows the Zulu "horns of the beast," enclosing the British position at Isandlwana. The central position of the Zulus, "the chest," was held by concentrated British fire, but as the British decided to reduce their overextended line and withdraw closer to the camp, they were overrun and the "horns" closed in.

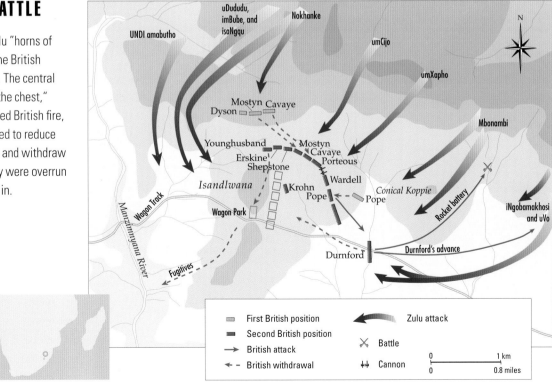

ISANDLWANA

THE BATTLEFIELD OF ISANDLWANA has changed little since the bloody events of 1879. The saddle-shaped mountain (known as a *nek*) towers over the ground at its base where Lord Chelmsford made his camp. Piles of whitewashed stones indicate where the bodies of British soldiers lay. It is a curiously intimate memorial—the huddles of stones signifying the last moments of groups of comrades, fighting for survival, and covering one another in the brutal struggle of hand-to-hand combat.

Right, *Romantic depiction of Melvill and Coghill,* defenders of the Queen's Colour, pursued by Zulus as they try to escape from Isandlwana. The two officers were posthumously awarded Victoria Crosses for their struggle to preserve the honor of the British Empire.

Below, *Under the relentless African sun, the white stone* of the burial markers that repeatedly dot the battlefield at Isandlwana add to the emotive atmosphere of this place.

Rorke's Drift

Wagon Track

FUGITIVES' DRIFT
The final fleeing soldiers were killed at Fugitives' Drift on the Buffalo River. Beside the river is a cross marking the spot where Melvill and Coghill died defending the Queen's Colour.

⑦ Melvill's Rock

Buffalo River

GETTING THERE

LOCATION: *KwaZulu-Natal, Republic of South Africa.*

VISITOR INFORMATION: *Isandlwana Lodge, P.O. Box 30, Isandlwana 3005 (e-mail isand@icon.co.za).*

TELEPHONE: *034 2718301*

DIRECTIONS: *North from Durban toward Dundee; turn east at Helpmekaar (three hours by car).*

TOUR DISTANCE: *11½ miles (18.5 km).*

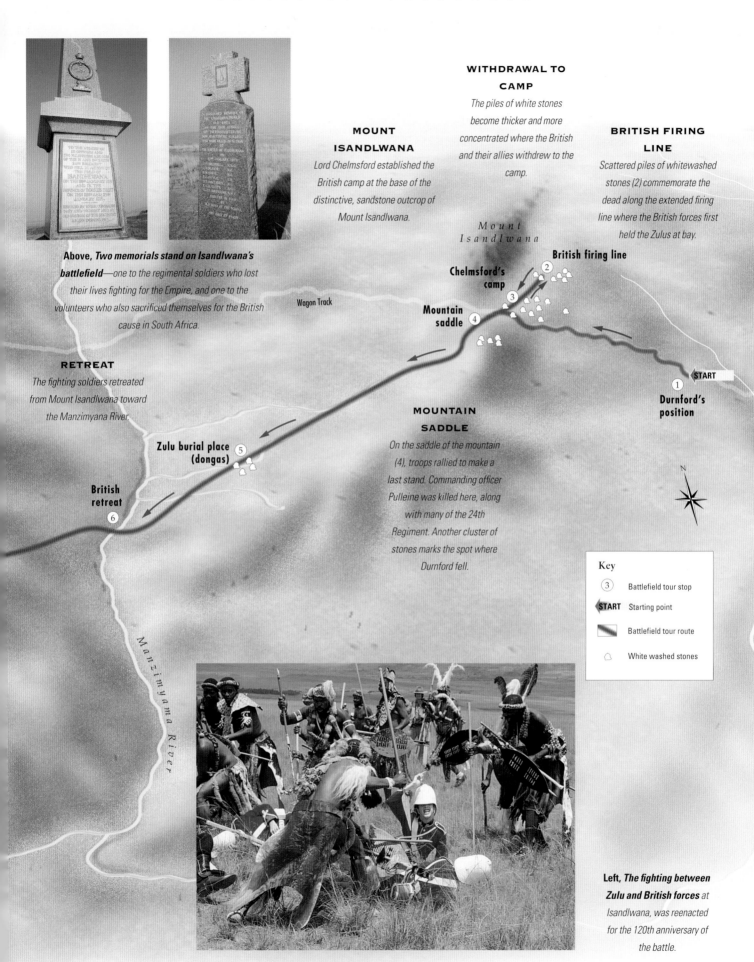

Above, *Two memorials stand on Isandlwana's battlefield*—one to the regimental soldiers who lost their lives fighting for the Empire, and one to the volunteers who also sacrificed themselves for the British cause in South Africa.

WITHDRAWAL TO CAMP

The piles of white stones become thicker and more concentrated where the British and their allies withdrew to the camp.

MOUNT ISANDLWANA

Lord Chelmsford established the British camp at the base of the distinctive, sandstone outcrop of Mount Isandlwana.

BRITISH FIRING LINE

Scattered piles of whitewashed stones (2) commemorate the dead along the extended firing line where the British forces first held the Zulus at bay.

Mount Isandlwana

British firing line

Chelmsford's camp

Wagon Track

Mountain saddle

RETREAT

The fighting soldiers retreated from Mount Isandlwana toward the Manzimyana River.

MOUNTAIN SADDLE

On the saddle of the mountain (4), troops rallied to make a last stand. Commanding officer Pulleine was killed here, along with many of the 24th Regiment. Another cluster of stones marks the spot where Durnford fell.

START

Durnford's position

Zulu burial place (dongas)

British retreat

Manzimyama River

Key

③	Battlefield tour stop
START	Starting point
▨	Battlefield tour route
⌂	White washed stones

Left, *The fighting between Zulu and British forces* at Isandlwana, was reenacted for the 120th anniversary of the battle.

MEHMETÇİĞE DERİN SAYGI

25 Nisan 1915 günü Conkbayırın da Türkler ve Birleşik Kuvvetleri arasında korkunç siper savaşları oluyor. Siperler arasında 8-10 m. mesafe var. Süngü hucumundan sonra savaşa ara verildi. Askerler siperlerine cekildi. Yaralılar ve ölüler toplanıyor. İki siper arasında açıkta ağır yaralı ve bir bacağı kopmak üzere olan İngiliz Yüzbaşısı avazı çıktığı kadar bağırıyor. ağlıyor. kurtarın diye yalvarıyordu. Ancak hiçbir siperden kimse çıkıp yardım edemiyor. Çünkü en küçük bir kıpırdanışta yüzlerce kurşun yağıyordu. Bu sırada akıl almaz bir olay oldu.

Türk siperlerinden beyaz bir iç çamaşırı sallandı. Arkasından arslan yapılı bir Türk askeri silahsız siperden çıktı. Hepimiz donup kaldık. Kimse nefes alamıyor ona bakıyorduk.

Asker yavaş adımlarla yürüyor siperdekiler kendisine nişan almış bekliyordu. Asker yaralı İngiliz subayını okşar gibi yerden kucakladı. kolunu omuzuna attı ve bizim siperlere doğru yürümeye başladı Yaralıyı usulca yere bırakıp geldiği gibi kendi siperlerine döndü teşekkür bile edemedik. Savaş alanlarında günlerce bu kahraman Türk askerlerinin cesareti güzelliği ve insan sevgisi konuşuldu.

Dünyanın en yürekli ve kahraman askeri mehmetçiğe derin sevgi ve saygılar.

üstegmen cosey
(Sonradan Avustralya Genel Valisi olmustur.)

DEATH IN THE SUN

Above, *British landing boats set off* from the River Clyde to participate in the landings at Cape Helles, on the tip of the Gallipoli peninsula.

Left, *the Turkish statue at Pine Ridge* commemorates a moment of compassion, when a Turkish soldier carried a wounded Australian officer back to the Anzac lines for treatment.

AS THE WAR ON THE WESTERN FRONT ground to a halt, with both sides entrenched behind barbed wire, it seemed a wise plan to move the impetus of the war against Germany to her weaker ally Turkey, against whom a far swifter and less costly campaign could be fought. As it happened, the campaign was neither fast nor effective—and a legend of tragedy and sacrifice was born.

AMPHIBIOUS CAMPAIGN

The original plan seemed remarkably simple, and it is easy to see how it gained support among Allied commanders. Sixteen British and French battleships would sail through the Dardanelles, silence the Turkish guns, bypass the Turkish army stationed there, and sail on to Istanbul to capture the Turkish capital. At first, all went well. From February 19 to March 18, the Allied battleships bombarded the Turkish positions on either side of the Dardanelles. They silenced most of the batteries, and the Turks were on the verge of defeat when three of the battleships suddenly hit mines and sank. Three more vessels were then disabled, and Rear Admiral

BACKGROUND TO BATTLE

Much was demanded from the Gallipoli campaign. Allied commanders could see that the war on the Western Front had bogged down, and that no breakthrough could be made there without an enormous cost in casualties.

As Lord of the Admiralty, Winston Churchill was one of the prime movers behind the campaign, seeing a way in which British naval expertise could be deployed to give strategic dynamism to the war.

Turkey was considered to be the sick man of Europe: an imperial power that was on its last legs, and could not withstand a determined attack by Western forces. By forcing its way through the Dardanelles, a British fleet could sail into the Sea of Marmara and capture the Turkish capital of Istanbul.

The removal of Turkey from the war would relieve pressure on Russia, who would no longer need to protect her southern borders, and could instead devote extra troops to attacking Germany.

A victory against Turkey would also encourage neutral eastern European powers, such as Romania, Bulgaria, and Greece, to enter the war against Austria and Germany.

SOUTH AUSTRALIANS

COO-EE!

FALL IN!

WE WANT **YOU** AT THE FRONT

COME AND HELP
ENLIST AT ONCE

John de Robeck swiftly withdrew his other craft. A landing of Allied troops on the Gallipoli peninsula was now thought necessary to help secure the passage of the ships.

A Mediterranean Expeditionary Force under the command of Sir Ian Hamilton was hastily assembled in Britain and Egypt. It comprised some 78,000 Allied soldiers, including large numbers of Australian and New Zealand volunteers, known as Anzacs. A month's delay in equipping the troops enabled the Turks to prepare their defenses fully on Gallipoli. Commanded by a German, General Otto Liman von Sanders, they numbered 60,000. The Allies landed on April 25, 1915 in two main assaults: one at Cape Helles, on the tip of the Gallipoli peninsula; and the other at Ari Burnu, on the west side of the peninsula. Two additional diversionary attacks were planned.

Because naval commanders were concerned about local currents and reefs, British troops landed at Cape Helles in daylight. As a result they hit the five chosen beaches under the full glare of the waiting Turkish gunners, who inflicted murderous fire upon them. Nevertheless, elements of the 29th Division pressed on bravely to capture a hill named Achi Baba. But, lacking firm orders from their commander, who was guiding events from offshore, they paused for a short break. By the time they resumed their attack, the Turks had occupied other high ground. They ringed the British with trenches, halting any additional advance and recreating the attrition warfare of the Western Front.

Farther north, the Anzacs had a better landing and quickly moved up the dusty slopes of the beaches, aiming for the high ground of Sari Bair. But the Turks in the area were commanded by the highly efficient Mustafa Kemal—later known as Kemal Ataturk, the founding President of the Turkish Republic. Kemal

LAUGHING AND JOKING

The Allies approached the landings at Gallipoli full of confidence in their military ability—but on the morning of April 25, they were in for a horrific shock. Captain Talbot, landing at Cape Helles with the 1st Battalion of the Lancashire Fusiliers, recalls the sense of levity:

I can tell you the sight of the peninsula being shelled by the fleet was grand with the sun rising above it all. We kicked off right outside the supporting ships and went in fairly fast until we were right under the cannon's mouth. The noise of the 10' etc were deafening. We never got a shot fired at us till the oars were tossed and then they started in earnest. The first bullet that struck the water brought up loud cheers from our men, but poor devils they little thought what they were in for .... Tom Mannsell and Tommy were shot getting out of the boat. Clark was shot through the head sitting in the boat .... I tell you I looked pretty slippy about getting ashore. I jumped overboard into five feet of water. I don't think the men realised how hot the fire was, they were still laughing and joking till the last.

Quoted in GREAT BATTLES OF THE GREAT WAR *by Michael Stedman (Pen & Sword, 1999).*

British troops wait in their landing craft *before approaching the beaches at Cape Helles. They landed in daylight and came under heavy Turkish fire.*

outdistanced the invaders and occupied the entire high ground with the Turkish 19th Division. At the end of the day, he launched a bitter counterattack, inflicting 5,000 casualties on the Anzacs and confining them to a tiny beachhead. Hamilton ordered them to stay. The Allies were now tortured by three months of hard fighting, blazing sun, and chronic dysentery.

SUVLA BAY

A breakout was essential, and three additional British divisions were sent to Gallipoli. The high ground of Sari Bair, above the area known as Anzac Cove, was the target. The landing took place under the cover of night on August 6–7, but without the support of battleships, as these had been forced into a safe harbor by German submarines. The new divisions landed at Suvla Bay, north of the Anzac position—it was left to the Anzacs to make the main assault on Sari Bair ridge. They lost their bearings in the dark, and the attack

Above, An Australian soldier.
Soldiers from Australia and New Zealand fought bravely, and felt let down by a British command that did not function effectively.

petered out, despite fierce hand-to-hand fighting with the Turks. The Suvla landing was a success, but the troops lacked orders about where to advance next—once again their delays allowed Turkish reinforcements to capture the high ground. Kemal launched a series of counterattacks, which pushed the Allies back to the beaches. Allied losses were 30,000.

Little had been achieved by the new offensive, and, as the fighting dragged on, Hamilton was finally relieved of his command in October. A new commander recommended the evacuation of all Allied troops from the peninsula, and this was achieved with no additional loss of life. The Allies had completely failed in their aim to knock Turkey out of the war—and had, in fact, encouraged an eastern European power, Bulgaria, to join with Germany.

Below, A British howitzer in action during the Gallipoli campaign. *Despite heavy bombardment, the Turks hung on to their rocky positions above the beaches.*

GALLIPOLI

ANZAC COVE IS AN UNLIKELY PLACE TO LAND TROOPS. Just yards from the beach, the ground rises in a succession of spectacular ridges and valleys. The experience of fighting across this landscape was recorded by a soldier of C Company, 11th Battalion, "The men … crawled, climbed, ran and struggled over boulders, hills, valleys and dales, ever going up and up this enormously high mountain like a cliff for it was a fearful height. Up and down we went, up, up, … to the summit which at last we reached and then we dashed along after the Turks …." Suddenly, the soldier recalls, there was a loud rumble, and the advance paused—it was gunfire from the ships in the bay, supporting the Commonwealth troops. The chase speeded up as the Turks quickly retreated.

The high ground described is Plugge's Plateau, which is dominated by a rocky outcrop known as the "Sphinx." The initial excitement of the landing gave way to a grim realization that the Turks would not be so easily moved from their positions on the summit of the ridges overlooking the Cove. Turkish counterattacks threw the Anzacs back to the coast, and the fighting settled into trench warfare.

As raid and counterraid failed to break the deadlock of fighting at Gallipoli, the soldiers began to suffer from another threat: the many bodies that lay unburied, and disease wiped out thousands of soldiers on both sides at Gallipoli.

PLAN OF BATTLE

The fighting from February to December, 1915 centered on the Gallipoli peninsula. The British held positions on the tip at Cape Helles, and the Australians and New Zealanders held positions on the west, at Anzac Cove. The Turks held the high ground, and kept the Allies pinned down on the beachheads with frequent counterattacks. The British fleet offered formidable supporting fire, but its role was diminished by the arrival of German submarines. A total of 410,000 British and Empire troops fought here, and there were 213,980 casualties, of which 145,000 were due to sickness.

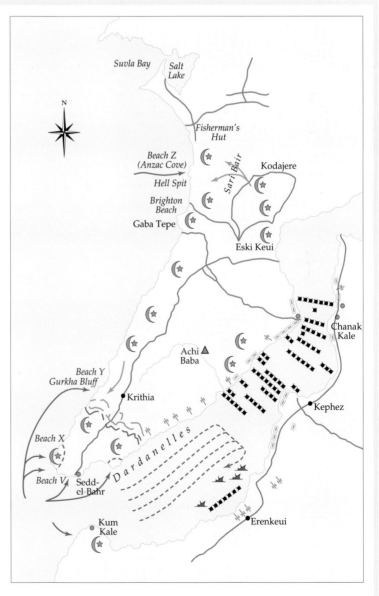

☾ Turkish forces	— Allied trenches	▲ Mountain/hill
→ Allied movements	— Turkish trenches	▭ Redoubt
⇢ Allied naval attacks	● Turkish forts	⊥ Battery
← Turkish movements	⚓ Ships sunk	■ Mine

0 2.5 miles
0 4 km

GALLIPOLI

VISIT THE BEACHES OF THE ALLIED LANDINGS on Gallipoli in the summer, and you get a taste of the formidable heat endured by the soldiers as they crouched on the sand and shingle beneath the Turkish positions high on the hills above. Yet this is also a place of great natural beauty, with an abundance of flowers and wildlife. A soldier who was there commented that it "would be quite divine without the war."

Above, _Ocean Beach_, one of the Allied landing spots north of Anzac Cove, revealing the harsh upland that faced Anzac troops advancing toward the Turkish positions on Sari Bair Ridge.

GETTING THERE

LOCATION: _Gallipoli (Geli Bolu) Peninsula, Turkey._

VISITOR INFORMATION: _Tourist Information, Valilik Binasi Kat 1, Canakkale._

TELEPHONE: _286 2171187_

DIRECTIONS: _180 miles (290 km) west of Istanbul. Narrow roads lead to Gaba Tepe; from there, explore Anzac Cove and inland; onto tip of peninsula for Cape Helles._

TOUR DISTANCE: _16 miles (10 km)._

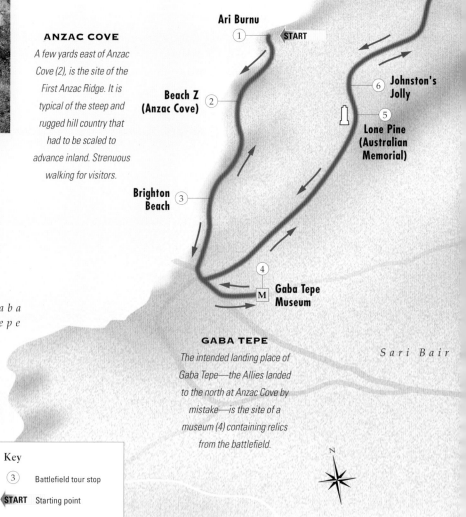

Suvla Bay

Salt Lake

Beach C

Beach B

Ocean Beach

AEGEAN SEA

Gaba Tepe

Sari Bair

SUVLA BAY
British landings at Suvla Bay on August 6 failed to capture the high ground, and met fierce Turkish counterattacks.

ARI BURNU
The main Australian and New Zealand landing took place at Ari Burnu (1), on beach Z. Rocks and cliffs made their advance difficult. The Anzac cemeteries are nearby.

The Nek ⑦

Ari Burnu
① ◀ **START**

ANZAC COVE
A few yards east of Anzac Cove (2), is the site of the First Anzac Ridge. It is typical of the steep and rugged hill country that had to be scaled to advance inland. Strenuous walking for visitors.

Beach Z (Anzac Cove) ②

Brighton Beach ③

⑥ **Johnston's Jolly**

⑤ **Lone Pine (Australian Memorial)**

④ **Gaba Tepe Museum** Ⓜ

GABA TEPE
The intended landing place of Gaba Tepe—the Allies landed to the north at Anzac Cove by mistake—is the site of a museum (4) containing relics from the battlefield.

Key

③ Battlefield tour stop

START Starting point

Battlefield tour route

⌂ Monument

Ⓜ Museum

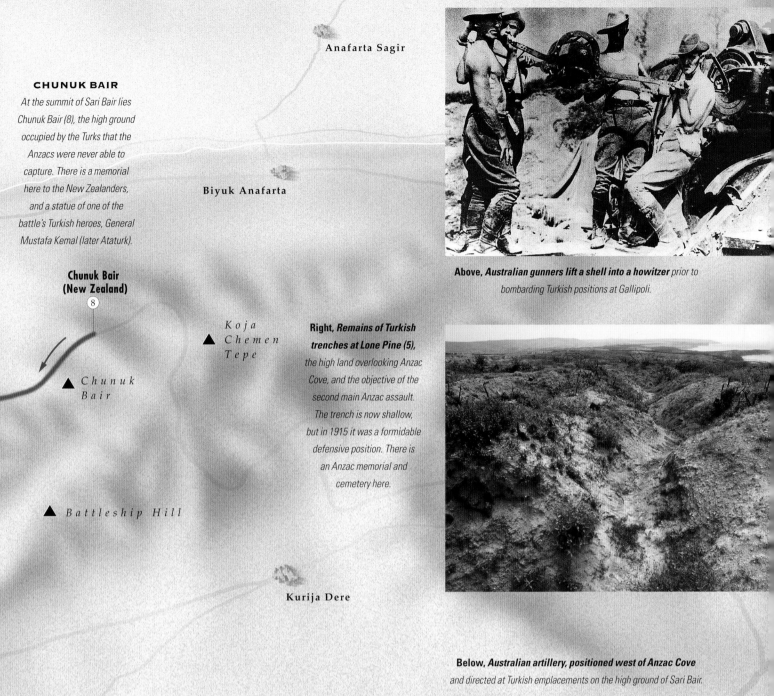

CHUNUK BAIR

At the summit of Sari Bair lies Chunuk Bair (8), the high ground occupied by the Turks that the Anzacs were never able to capture. There is a memorial here to the New Zealanders, and a statue of one of the battle's Turkish heroes, General Mustafa Kemal (later Ataturk).

Anafarta Sagir

Biyuk Anafarta

Chunuk Bair (New Zealand)
(8)

▲ *Koja Chemen Tepe*

▲ *Chunuk Bair*

▲ *Battleship Hill*

Kurija Dere

Eski Keui

Above, *Australian gunners lift a shell into a howitzer* prior to bombarding Turkish positions at Gallipoli.

Right, *Remains of Turkish trenches at Lone Pine (5)*, the high land overlooking Anzac Cove, and the objective of the second main Anzac assault. The trench is now shallow, but in 1915 it was a formidable defensive position. There is an Anzac memorial and cemetery here.

Below, *Australian artillery, positioned west of Anzac Cove* and directed at Turkish emplacements on the high ground of Sari Bair.

DAY OF INFAMY

Above, *A Japanese aerial photograph* taken during the attack
shows Ford Island and the vulnerable U.S. warships moored around it.

Left, *The National Memorial Cemetery* at Punchbowl in Honolulu.

P EARL HARBOR IS A NATURAL INLET with protected shallow water, on
the island of Oahu, in Hawaii. Since April 1940, the U.S. Pacific
Fleet had based its headquarters there with the aim of dissuading
aggressive moves by the Japanese Navy in the Pacific. On November 11,
1940, on the other side of the world, British planes had flown from the
aircraft-carrier *Illustrious* and devastated the Italian fleet at Taranto,
paralyzing the Italian Navy. This event made little impact on U.S. Navy
staff, but the easy victory was studied closely by other military leaders—
notably the Japanese Admiral Isoruku Yamamoto.

FIRST STRIKE

Yamamoto was convinced that Japan could never beat the United States in
a long war—it did not have the industrial capacity or natural resources. He
opposed war with the U.S. but, compelled by duty, came up with a plan—
a massive surprise blow that would force the Americans to negotiate a
favorable peace. Other Japanese military leaders disagreed, arguing that
such an attack would outrage the U.S. and make it determined to fight a
long war, whereas a strike against the European empires would be far less
bitter and result in a compromise. Yamamoto would not be persuaded, and
threatened several times to resign. Eventually, in fall 1941, the Japanese
Imperial staff gave in. On November 26, six aircraft carriers, two battle-

BACKGROUND TO BATTLE

In 1905, Japan shocked the world by defeating the Russian Empire. Japan was officially acknowledged as a great power, and embarked on an expansion of her own empire in southern Asia.

Japan entered World War I on the Allied side and swiftly seized several German concessions and territories abroad.

Japanese troops overran Manchuria in 1931, and ruthlessly invaded China in 1937. Hundreds of thousands of Chinese were killed, and a puppet Chinese government was established.

In 1940, following France's defeat by Germany, Japan invaded French Indochina. The U.S. government warned Japan against this move, and placed an embargo on steel bound for Japan. On September 27, Japan signed an alliance with Nazi Germany and Fascist Italy.

From September 1941, U.S. pilots formed the American Volunteer Group, or "Flying Tigers," to help the Chinese fight Japanese occupation. In October, Lieutenant General Hideki Tojo took over the Japanese government and initiated plans for war against the British, the Dutch, and the Americans.

ships, and escorting cruisers and destroyers led by Vice Admiral Chuichi Nagumo, left the Kurile Islands for Hawaii.

The situation between the United States and Japan was tense, following Japan's continued fighting in China and a U.S. embargo on the importation of strategic materials to Japan. But U.S. intelligence could not crack Japanese naval or military codes to obtain any precise information on Japanese movements. On November 26, the U.S. Secretary of State rejected proposals from Japanese diplomats in Washington, and subsequently a war warning was sent to Admiral Husband E. Kimmel, commander of the Pacific Fleet: "An aggressive move is expected within the next few days." said the message, "Organization of naval task forces indicates an amphibious expedition against either the Philippines, Thai or Kra peninsula or possibly Borneo. Execute appropriate defensive deploy-

Above, *Damaged U.S. warships,* *including the destroyers* Downes *and* Cassin, *with the battleship* Pennsylvania *in the background. The attack on Pearl Harbor was very effective, but only in the short term. The United States soon recovered to continue their battle against the Axis powers .*

ment." All of this was a long way from Hawaii.

The Japanese fleet drew closer to Hawaii, and two messages sent from Tokyo to the Japanese ambassador in Washington indicated an imminent assault on Pearl Harbor. U.S.intelligence was still not prepared for war, however, and a delay in communicating this information to Pearl Harbor meant that it was not received in time. A U.S. radar operator on Oahu spotted Japanese aircraft nearby, but was reassured that this was unimportant. Finally, the sinking of a Japanese midget submarine outside Pearl Harbor failed to bring a general alert. The U.S. Navy was sleepwalking to disaster.

"TORA! TORA! TORA!"

On the morning of December 7, Nagumo positioned his fleet 275 miles (442 km) north of Oahu. His air power was formidable: 104 Nakajima B5N2 torpedo bombers, 135 Aichi

AND THE BAND PLAYED ON . . .

Japanese planes prepare to take off from an aircraft carrier at sea. It was the long-range use of aircraft carriers that enabled the Japanese to attack Pearl Harbor.

As the first wave of Japanese aircraft attacked Pearl Harbor, Oden McMillan was conducting a Marine band on the U.S. battleship *Nevada*. As they played the "Star-Spangled Banner," a Japanese plane shot up the ship around them:

McMillan knew now [that they were being attacked], but kept on conducting. The years of training had taken over—it never occurred to him that once he had begun playing the National Anthem he could possibly stop. Another strafer flashed by. This time McMillan unconsciously paused as the deck splintered around him, but he quickly picked up the beat again. The entire band stopped and started again with him, as though they had rehearsed it for weeks. Not a man broke formation until the final note ended. Then everyone ran wildly for cover.

From DAY OF INFAMY *by Walter Lord
(Holt, Rinehart & Winston, 1957).*

Left, *U.S. battleships* West Virginia *and* Tennessee *burn after being hit by Japanese bombs in the first-wave attack on Pearl Harbor.*

D3A1 dive-bombers, and 81 Mitsubishi A6M2 Zero fighters. At 6:00 A.M. he sent his first wave of aircraft toward Pearl Harbor. Two hours later, in clear, early morning light, the Japanese aircraft dropped their bombs on the U.S. fleet moored alongside Ford Island. The torpedoes were especially modified to function in the shallow harbor, and there were no torpedo nets in the water to intercept them. The destruction was enormous. The *Arizona*, *Oklahoma*, *West Virginia*, and *California* were all hit and sunk. Sleepy airforce and navy crew could offer little resistance to the first attack. U.S. aircraft parked on five airfields in Oahu were almost all destroyed or severely damaged, stopping U.S. pilots from facing the Japanese in the air. "Tora! Tora! Tora!" screamed the Japanese pilots, elated by their easy victory—"Tora" means Tiger, and was the code used to launch the attack.

Three-quarters of an hour later, a second wave of Japanese aircraft roared across Pearl Harbor, delivering more destruction. Four more battleships were damaged. The smoke billowing upward from the burning ships hampered the precision of the second-wave aircraft, but over 3,000 U.S. servicemen were killed, and the Pacific Fleet lost 18 ships and 187 aircraft in an attack that lasted no longer than two hours.

It was a remarkable Japanese triumph, and immediately won Yamamoto what he wanted; the U.S. Pacific Fleet was neutralized for at least six months. But three U.S. aircraft carriers were absent from Pearl Harbor, and the shallow water meant that many of the ships could be raised and repaired. Also, the Japanese declaration of war, which was supposed to reach their delegates in Washington at the same time that Nagumo received his order to attack, was delayed, so the strike occurred prior to war being declared. Although, the United States had been stung by this "date which will live in infamy," as President Roosevelt called it, they went on to fight a determined and destructive war against Japan which eventually brought Japan's complete defeat.

PEARL HARBOR

ON THAT FATEFUL DAY at Pearl Harbor, U.S.S. *Arizona* was part of "Battleship Row"—on the south side of Ford Island stood seven of the U.S. Pacific Fleet's eight battleships. Japanese air commander Mitsuo Fuchida, flying over the harbor, could not believe the battleships' proximity to each other: "Even in the deepest peace, I have never seen ships anchored at a distance of less than 500 to 1,000 yards from each other. The picture down there was hard to comprehend."

Torpedoes from Japanese bombers were the main cause of destruction. The *Nevada* suffered a vast hole in its port bow. The *Arizona* exploded like a fireworks display, ignited by torpedoes and a bomb. At least six torpedoes hit the *West Virginia*, which slowly sank to the bottom of the harbor. The *Oklahoma* was also hit several times by torpedoes and began

Above, *Admiral Isoruku Yamamoto,* *commander of the Japanese Imperial Navy, conceived the attack on Pearl Harbor in order to try and dissuade the United States from going to war with Japan.*

to keel over. The *California* was struck twice. The *Maryland* and the *Tennessee*, protected from torpedoes by the outer ships and Ford Island, were hit by high-level bombs. Fire from the *Arizona* spread to the *Tennessee*. The eighth battleship, the *Pennsylvania*, was in dry dock and hit by only one bomb.

The devastation was not as great as it first appeared, and did not knock the United States out of the war in one blow, as was intended. Of the eight battleships attacked, only the *Arizona* and the *Oklahoma* would never sail again. The aircraft and smaller ships could be replaced, and no aircraft carriers or submarines were destroyed. Although shocked by the loss of life and the surprise of the attack, the U.S. was more than ready to strike back.

PLAN OF BATTLE

The U.S. Pacific Fleet was moored around Ford Island at Pearl Harbor on Sunday, December 7, 1941. Japanese aircraft attacked in two waves, from 8:00 A.M. onward. Five U.S. battleships took direct hits: the *West Virginia, Arizona, Nevada, Oklahoma,* and *California*. The *Nevada* tried to escape by steaming out of the harbor, but was hit repeatedly. Rather than allow the vessel to sink, and block the harbor entrance, the captain took the difficult decision to beach her.

Key to ships

1	Oklahoma
2	West Virginia
3	Ramapo
4	New Orleans
5	San Francisco
6	Honolulu
→	Japanese air attack
⬭	Ship destroyed
⬭	Ship damaged

```
0                    1 mile
0                   1.6 km
```

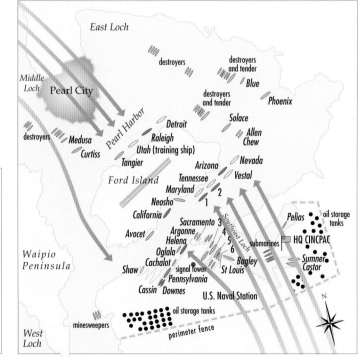

PEARL HARBOR

EARL HARBOR IS STILL a United States naval base, but at its heart is the U.S.S. *Arizona* Memorial, floating above the remains of the battleship—more than 1,000 members of her crew who died aboard the vessel remain buried inside. The Stars and Stripes is raised and lowered over the memorial every day. Nearby is the U.S.S. *Bowfin* Submarine Museum and Park.

Above, *U.S. troops* *try to defend an airfield against the Japanese attack. Oahu's airfields were set alight by Japanese bombs, and the belching fires and smoke hindered the second Japanese attack.*

99

PEARL CITY

East Loch

Pearl Harbor

FORD ISLAND

Lexington Boulevard

U.S.S. *Missouri*

Southeast Loch

U.S.S.
Arizona
Memorial

GETTING THERE

LOCATION: *Pearl Harbor, Oahu, Hawaii.*

VISITOR INFORMATION: *U.S.S. Arizona Memorial, 1 Arizona Memorial Place, Honolulu, HA 96818-3145.*

TELEPHONE: *808- 422- 2771.*

DIRECTIONS: *By bus: No. 20 from Waikiki to Memorial bus stop. By car: from Honolulu take Highway 1 past Honolulu airport, across Makai Viaduct; then enter Kamehameha Highway 99, following signs to Pearl Harbor Visitor Center.*

TOUR DISTANCE: *3 miles (4.75 km).*

Right, *The U.S.S.* **Arizona Memorial (2),** *built above the remains of the battleship, is dedicated to over 1,000 U.S. Service personnel who still lay buried in the wreck of the ship. This is one of the most visited sites in Hawaii, and line-ups are likely.*

AIEA

U.S.S. BOWFIN SUBMARINE MUSEUM AND PARK

Located next to the U.S.S. Arizona Memorial Visitor Center, this museum (3) takes an extended look at the fascinating history of submarines and provides an opportunity for visitors to go below deck.

Aloha Stadium

VISITOR CENTER

Inside Pearl Harbor naval base is the Visitor Center (1), where a movie recounts the story of the Japanese raid on Pearl Harbor. Tickets can be obtained here for the shuttle boat to the Arizona Memorial.

Kamehameha Highway

99

Admiral Clarey Bridge (Ford Island Bridge)

McGrew Point Naval Housing

U.S.S. Bowfin and Submarine Park ③ ①

U.S.S. Arizona Memorial Visitor Center

START

Ferry

Makalapa Park

Kamehameha Highway

Pearl Harbor Naval Reservation

Below, *U.S. Navy personnel place wreaths* *on the graves of comrades killed in the Japanese attack.*

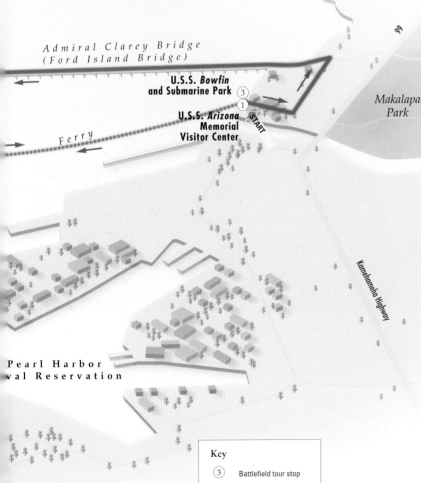

Key

③ Battlefield tour stop

START Starting point

　 Battlefield tour route

SIEGE IN VIETNAM

Above, *The Foreign Legion in French Indochina* in the 1950s formed the
backbone of the French stand at Dien Bien Phu.

Left, *A view westward from Eliane* toward the airstrip in the center of Dien
Bien Phu. It shows the natural basin that the French had to defend against the Viet
Minh who were based on the high ground around it.

BACKGROUND TO BATTLE

The Japanese defeat of the
British and other Westerners in
Southeast Asia during World War
II encouraged native nationalist
movements to challenge their
colonial rulers in the years
immediately after the war.

In Vietnam, Ho Chi Minh
proclaimed the Vietnam Republic
on September 2, 1945. Thus began
one of the longest and bitterest
military contests of the second
half of the twentieth century.

At first, the French recognized the
republic as a free state within its
own Indochinese federation, but
the Viet Minh wanted more—and
began guerrilla warfare.

Trained in China and recognized
by both the Communist Chinese
and the Russians, the Viet Minh
inflicted several defeats on the
French from 1950 onward.

In December 1950, Marshal Jean
de Lattre de Tassigny was put in
command of French forces. He
managed to restore French rule,
but continuing guerrilla warfare
won more political concessions
from the French, and the Viet
Minh could see no reason for
halting their activity.

In January 1953, a French naval
raid damaged rebel bases, and a
knockout blow at Dien Bien Phu
was planned for November.

AFTER WORLD WAR II, nationalist groups across Southeast Asia aimed
to seize power from their colonial rulers, and end the European
empire in the Far East. Their most effective method was guerrilla
warfare. In Vietnam it had been mastered by the Viet Minh, whose military
leader was Vo Nguyen Giap. The French colonial rulers of Vietnam were
determined to draw the Viet Minh into a major battle, where they hoped
their superior military skills would overwhelm the guerrillas.

AIRSTRIP IN THE JUNGLE

The chosen point of confrontation was Dien Bien Phu, a village 220 miles
(354 km) west of Hanoi near the border with Laos. At its center was an
airstrip, which the French hoped would keep them supplied while they
drew the Viet Minh onto their guns and fought an aggressive siege. Such
tactics had worked in the same part of Vietnam 70 years earlier, when a
French garrison successfully resisted the onslaught of native guerrillas. But
this time, the French seriously underestimated their opponents.

The French, commanded by Brigadier-General Christian de la Croix
de Castries, numbered just over 10,000 men, including elite French

Foreign Legionnaires. They arranged their guns—24 105-mm and four 155-mm howitzers—and ten M-24 light tanks on their perimeter, in code-named strongpoints. The Viet Minh, commanded by Giap, assembled more than 37,000 troops and over 200 pieces of artillery, including rocket launchers and anti-aircraft guns. French troops were parachuted into Dien Bien Phu on November 20, 1953, but the fighting did not begin until the following February, with the sporadic artillery bombardment of French positions.

Giap began the main Viet Minh assault on March 13 by aiming a heavy bombardment at strongpoint *Beatrice*. The artillery tore the position apart, wrecking the defenses; but the Foreign Legionnaires based there held on for over eight hours until de Castries ordered them to retreat. The Viet Minh moved on to strongpoint *Gabrielle*, held by Algerian troops and a Foreign Legion mortar unit. De Castries would not yield this position so easily, and ordered a counterattack by two companies of Legion paratroopers, some Indochinese soldiers, and M-24 tanks. They had reached the Nam Yum

Above, *The 155-mm howitzer used by the French*—still in the position it occupied during the battle. Its commander killed himself with a hand-grenade.

HEROISM IS NOT ENOUGH

The French fought fiercely at Dien Bien Phu, and felt disillusioned by the result of their sacrifice. A French paratroop commander summed up his feelings to a journalist:

It was all for nothing. I let my men die for nothing. The Viets [Viet Minh] told us they had won because they were fighting for an ideal, and we were not. I told them about my paras at Dien Bien Phu. I told them how they fought, and they said "Heroism is no answer." Dien Bien Phu was not an accident of fate. It was a judgement.

Quoted in TO THE LAST CARTRIDGE *by Robert Barr Smith (Avon Books, 1994).*

A Vietnamese memorial shows de Castries emerging from his bunker to surrender on May 7, 1954.

Left, ***The bridge across the Nam Yum River*** *in the center of Dien Bien Phu, now a peaceful country town.*

Below, ***The banks of the Nam Yum River*** *became home to many French deserters who were known as "the Rats of Nam Yum."*

River, which bisected the area, when they came under heavy artillery fire.

The Indochinese scattered; one tank was knocked out, and the rest retreated. Only the Legionnaires pressed on, determined to rescue their comrades. But they were too few, and, despite their bravery, they were later forced to abandon this position also. Giap now had command of the high ground above Dien Bien Phu and could turn his guns with ease on its defenders.

AIR DROPS

Continuing his step-by-step reduction of Dien Bien Phu, Giap launched an attack on *Anne-Marie*. On March 17, its defenders deserted en masse, and the strongpoint was overrun. By March 23, the airstrip was captured, and Viet Minh trenches dug to within rifle shot of the remaining French strongholds. Supplies had to be dropped by air, but many of these ended in the wrong hands, and French aircraft suffered terribly at the hands of Viet Minh anti-aircraft guns—at least 62 aircraft were shot down. Before abandoning the airstrip, the French ripped out some of its steel reinforcements and incorporated them into their own fortified positions—these are still visible today in de Castries' headquarters.

At the beginning of April, the Viet Minh led a fierce assault against *Isabelle*. French reinforcements were flown in at night, but many of the Legion paratroopers were killed in the air, or landed among the enemy. Under increasing pressure, North African troops deserted the position, leaving the Legionnaires to take up the defense. They held on for a month amid bitter fighting.

Above, De Castries' command bunker—occupied throughout the battle—is located near the airstrip, and can be visited as part of the museum tour.

The principal Vietnamese memorial to the victory at Dien Bien Phu, which stands outside the town's museum.

Elsewhere, *Eliane* (under assault since March) hung on—finally falling on May 6. *Huguette* and *Claudine* came under heavy attack. The situation was desperate. De Castries could see no way out, and on May 7 decided to surrender his command post. *Isabelle* fell that evening, after the French there staged a brave breakout. Giap achieved a tremendous victory that effectively ended French rule in Vietnam, but at the cost of at least 8,000 dead and 15,000 wounded. The French lost 4,000 dead, and the remainder were led into captivity—from which few returned.

Right, The M-24 light tank, nicknamed "Bison," used by the French in their counterattacks against the Viet Minh. It was airdropped, and assembled by the soldiers on the ground. The tank is one of many artifacts that remain on the actual battlefield.

DIEN BIEN PHU

THE MOST PROMINENT FEATURE at Dien Bien Phu is the strongpoint known as *Eliane*, where the Vietnamese located their memorial. This was the position that resulted in so much bloodshed and sacrifice. Memorials dot the scene, recording the French units who held it: the 3rd T'ai Battalion and the 5th Vietnamese Parachute Battalion, replaced by the 1st Battalion, 4th Moroccan Tirailleurs, a company of the 8th Parachute Assault Battalion, and a company of engineers. Visitors can enter the French bunkers, which are preserved intact with concrete sandbags, but they are warned to beware of the snakes that have made their home there.

From the top of *Eliane*, you can look down at the valley and see the airstrip in the middle, and other positions around it. To the west of the airstrip, in the town center, is the site of de Castries' headquarters. The headquarters are fenced off with barbed wire, but they can be viewed as part of an official tour of the museum and key sites. The museum is one large room, containing photographs and items of military memorabilia retrieved from the battlefield. Outside the museum are a number of artillery pieces. The tour includes a visit to the Vietnamese graveyard.

The center of the valley now consists of rice fields, and can be very muddy to cross. French tanks and pieces of artillery can be found here, mounted on concrete blocks. *Dominique* is the highest of the French strongpoints, and also offers an excellent view of the valley. Artillery observers were located here.

Elsewhere in the valley, strongpoint *Juno* is marked by the remains of a heavy machine-gun mount. *Isabelle* is situated about 3 miles (5 km) outside Dien Bien Phu, but is covered in heavy brush and is arduous to visit.

PLAN OF BATTLE

Dien Bien Phu is in a basin through which the Nam Yum River runs. French strongpoints, which were given French female names, formed a defensive ring around the airstrip in the middle. When the Viet Minh began knocking out the strongpoints and captured the high ground, they were able to subject the French positions to overwhelming bombardment.

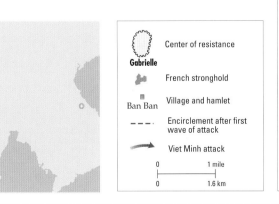

Center of resistance
Gabrielle

French stronghold

Village and hamlet
Ban Ban

- - - Encirclement after first wave of attack

Viet Minh attack

0   1 mile
0   1.6 km

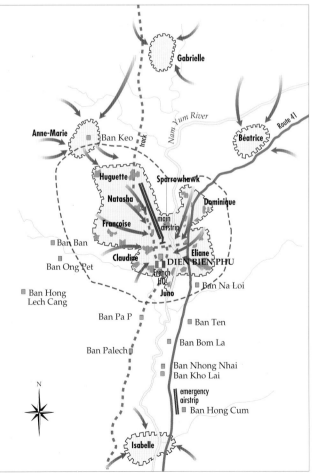

DIEN BIEN PHU

IEN BIEN PHU IS A GROWING TOWN in northwest Vietnam, surrounded by jungle. It is not easy to reach, and visitors need to take a guide from Hanoi or to join an organized tour. Having made the journey, the visitor will be rewarded with many relics of the epic battle fought there.

Above, *Looking south from Eliane* *along the basin of Dien Bien Phu toward Isabelle. Eliane, on high ground, was fiercely defended by the French until the bitter end.*

Below, *A Vietnamese memorial to the French* *who fought at Eliane, showing their various unit badges, including that of the Foreign Legion.*

AIRSTRIP
The airstrip (5) lay at the center of the French position. By March 23, 1954, the Viet Minh had closed it to French air support. There are plans to reopen the airstrip for tourists from Hanoi. De Castries' headquarters bunker, still visible today, is located near the airstrip.

Ban Keo

Huguette

Natasha

Françoise

Claudine

main airstrip

5

4

DIEN BIEN PHU

Juno

Nam Yum River

Ban Pa Pé

Ban Ten

GETTING THERE

LOCATION: *Dien Bien Phu, northwest Vietnam.*

VISITOR INFORMATION: *Vietnam Tourism,
80 Quan Su, Hanoi
(e-mail: TITC@vietnamtourism.com).*

TELEPHONE: *84-4-8252246*

DIRECTIONS: *220 miles west of Hanoi. It is
recommended to hire a guide and Jeep in Hanoi, or
to join an organized tour.*

TOUR DISTANCE: *12 miles (19.5 km)*

Right, *A row of Viet Minh
artillery outside the museum
at Dien Bien Phu (4). Giap
used the numerical superiority
of his big guns to devastating
effect against the French.*

Gabrielle

BEATRICE AND GABRIELLE

*The French strongpoints of Beatrice
and Gabrielle were the first points
of attack by the Viet Minh, and were
captured in mid-March.*

Nam Yum River

① Béatrice

START

Route 41

② Dominique

DOMINIQUE AND ELIANE

*Dominique and Eliane (3) came under
sustained attack from mid-March, but
Eliane held out fiercely until the end.
There is a museum, memorials, and a
military graveyard near Eliane, and
many French bunkers also survive.*

Mt. Fictif

Below, *French Foreign Legionnaires on
a supply truck in Indochina in the 1950s.*

M ③ Elaine

Route 41

Mt. Chauve

Ban Na Loi

Key

③ Battlefield tour stop

START Starting point

Monument

M Museum

Battlefield tour route

N

TOUR OPERATORS, ORGANIZATIONS, AND MUSEUMS

BATTLEFIELD TOUR OPERATORS

BATTLEFIELDS AFRICA
BOX 2388, Hillcrest 2350, South Africa
Contact: Ron Lock
Fax: 031 765 1244
Zulu, Boer, and South African Wars; professional guide.

CONNECTION GROUP TOURS
101 Duncan Mill Road, Suite 305, Don Mills, Ontario, M3B 1Z3, Canada
Website: www.connectiongrouptours.com
Telephone: 416-449-4652; 877-449-4652
Fax: 416-449-9965
E-mail: grouptours@connectiongrouptours.com
Focuses on North America's involvement in World War I and World War II in Europe.

GALINA INTERNATIONAL BATTLEFIELD TOURS
1 Tokenspire Business Park, Woddmansey, Beverley, Humberside HU17 0TB, U.K.
Contact: Barry Matthews
Telephone: 01482 804409
Fax: 01482 809717
Official tour operators for Normandy Veterans' Association. Destinations include Western Front, Dunkirk, Normandy, Arnhem, Italy, and Gallipoli.

HISTORIC ZULULAND TOURS
49 Belsize Park, London NW3 4EE, U.K.
Contact: Ian Castle
Zulu War tours.

HOLTS' TOURS (BATTLEFIELDS & HISTORY)
15 Market Street, Sandwich, Kent CT13 9DA, U.K.
Website: www.battletours.co.uk
Contact: John Hughes-Wilson
E-mail: info@holts.co.uk
Telephone: 01304 612248
Fax: 01304 614930
Biggest military historical tour operator, with program spanning history from the Romans to the Falklands War. Especially well known for World War I and World War II battlefield tours.

IAN FLETCHER BATTLEFIELD TOURS
PO BOX 112, Rochester, Kent ME1 2EX, U.K.
Contact: Ian Fletcher
Telephone: 016034 319973
Fax: 01634 324263
Peninsular War and Waterloo tours.

MIDAS HISTORICAL TOURS LTD
Halland House, 66 York Road, Weybridge, Surrey KT13 9DY, U.K.
Website: www.midastours.co.uk
Contact: Alan Rooney
Telephone: 01932 831155
Fax: 01932 831156
Escorted tours covering ancient and medieval warfare, Napoleonic, American Civil War, South Africa, India, Crimea, World War I, and World War II.

MIDDLEBROOK-HODGSON BATTLEFIELD TOURS
48 Linden Way, Boston, Lincolnshire PE21 9DS, U.K.
Telephone: 01526 342249
Fax: 01526 345249
Tours to World War I Western Front, Ypres to Verdun, Normandy, and Gallipoli.

OLD COUNTRY TOURS INC.

P.O. BOX 340, Flourtown, Pennsylvania 19031-0340, U.S.A.
P.O. Box 324, Esher, Surrey, KT10 0XD, U.K.
Website: www.oldcountrytours.com
Contact: Peter Gascoyne-Lockwood
Telephone: 800-953-5812 (U.S.A.); 020 8398 5368 (U.K.)
Fax: 020 8398 5594 (U.K.)
E-mail: info@oldcountrytours.com
Tours of all historical battlefields in the U.S.A. and Europe.

SALIENT TOURS

Gwalia House, Dinas, Trelech, Carmarthenshire, Wales SA33 6SE, U.K.
Website: www.battlefields.freeserve.co.uk
Contact: Mark Horner
Telephone: 01994 484717
E-mail: tours@battlefields.freeserve.co.uk
Daily battlefield tours of Ypres and the Somme.

SOCIETY OF FRIENDS OF THE NATIONAL ARMY MUSEUM

National Army Museum, Royal Hospital Road, London SW3 4HT, U.K.
Contact: Derek A. Mumford
Telephone/fax: 020 7730 0717
Organizes tours to foreign battlefields.

SOMME BATTLEFIELD TOURS LTD

19 Old Road, Wimborne, Dorset, England BH21 1EJ, U.K.
Website: www.btinternet.com/~sommetours/index.html
Contact: James Power
Telephone/fax: 01202 840520
Specializes in taking small groups to all the major sites as well as off the beaten track around the battlefields of the Somme.

UK TOURS & TRAVEL

131 Blackburn Road, Bolton, Lancashire BC1 8HF, U.K.
Contact: Peter and Angela Smith
Telephone/fax: 00 44 1204 384940
American Civil War battlefield tours.

THE WAR RESEARCH SOCIETY BATTLEFIELD AND MEMORIAL PILGRIMAGE TOURS

The War Research Society, 27 Courtway Avenue, Birmingham B14 4PP, U.K.
Contact: Ian C. Alexander
Telephone: 0121 430 5348
Fax: 0121 436 7401
Battlefield tours all over Europe and of the Boer/Zulu wars battlefields.

BATTLEFIELD ORGANIZATIONS

ENGLISH HERITAGE

Portland House, Stag Place, London SW1E 5EE, U.K.
Website: www.english-heritage.org.uk
Telephone: 020 7973 3434
Administers English battlefields and organizes events on these sites.

NATIONAL PARK SERVICE

U.S. Department of the Interior
Website: www.nps.gov
Administers U.S. National Military Parks.

BATTLEFIELD MUSEUMS

BELGIUM

BASTOGNE HISTORICAL CENTER
Colline du Mardasson, B-6600, Bastogne
Telephone: 061 211413
Fax: 061 217373

IN FLANDERS FIELDS
Lakenhallen-Grote Markt 34, B-8900 Ieper
Website: www.inflandersfield.be
E-mail: flandersfield@ieper.be
Telephone: 057 22 85 84
Fax: 057 21 85 89

ENGLAND

HASTINGS CASTLE
West Hill, Hastings, East Sussex
Telephone: 01424 781112

FRANCE

BATTERIE DE LONGUES
14400 Longues-sur-Mer, Normandy
Telephone: 031 06 06 45

MUSÉE AMERICA GOLD BEACH
Place Admiral Byrd, 14114 Ver-Sur-Mer, Normandy
Telephone: 031 22 58 58

MUSÉE DE LA BATTERIE DE MERVILLE
14810 Merville-Franceville, Normandy
Telephone: 031 24 21 83

MUSÉE DES ABRIS SOMME 1916
Rue Eruanicet, Godin, 80300 Albert
E-mail; cityweb@nnx.com
Telephone: 03 22 75 1617
Fax: 03 22 64 0046

MUSÉE DES ÉPAVES SOUS-MARINES DU DÉBARQUEMENT
Route de Bayeux, Commes, 14520 Port-en-Bessin, Normandy
Telephone: 031 21 17 06

MUSÉE DES RANGERS
Quai Crampon, 14450 Grandcamp-Maisy, Normandy
Telephone: 031 92 33 51

MUSÉE DU DÉBARQUEMENT
Place du 6 Juin, 14117 Arromanches, Normandy
Telephone: 031 22 34 31
Fax: 031 92 68 83

MUSÉE DU MUR DE L'ATLANTIQUE
Avenue du 6 Juin, 14150 Ouistreham, Normandy
Telephone: 031 97 28 69
Fax: 031 96 66 05

MUSÉE MEMORIAL DE LA BATAILLE DE NORMANDIE
Boulevard Fabian Ware, 14400 Bayeux, Normandy
Telephone: 031 92 93 41
Fax: 031 21 85 11

MUSÉE MEMORIAL DU GENERAL DE GAULLE
10 rue Bourbesneur, 14400 Bayeux
Telephone: 031 92 45 55

MUSÉE NO. 4 COMMANDO
Place Alfred Thomas, 14150 Ouistreham, Normandy
Telephone: 031 96 63 10

MUSÉE OMAHA 6 JUIN 1944
Rue de la Mer, 14710 Saint-Laurent-Sur-Mer, Normandy
Telephone: 031 21 97 44
Fax: 031 92 72 80

MUSEUM OF THE GREAT WAR IN PERONNE
Chateau de Peronne, B.P. 63, 80201 Peronne
Telephone: 03 22 83 14 18
Fax: 03 22 83 54 18

SOUTH AFRICA

ANGLO-BOER WAR MUSEUM
100 Monument Road, Bloemfontein 9301
Website: www.anglo-boer.co.za
E-mail: museum@anglo-boer.co.za
Telephone: 051 447 3447
Fax: 051 447 1322

TALANA MUSEUM
P.B. 2024, Dundee 3000
Website: www.talana.co.za
E-mail: info@talana.co.za
Telephone: 034 212 2654
Fax: 034 212 2376

TURKEY

GABA TEPE MUSEUM—KABATEPE MUZE VE TANITMA MERKEZI
Gelibolu Yarmadasi, Eceabat, Canakkale
Telephone: 286-8141297

NAVAL MUSEUM
Cimenlik Kalesi (Cimenlik Park), Canakkale
Telephone: 286-8620082

U.S.A.

THE ALAMO MUSEUM
The Alamo, 300 Alamo Plaza, San Antonio, Texas 78299-2599
Telephone: 210-225-1391
Fax: 210-229-1343

BATTLESHIP MISSOURI MEMORIAL
P.O. Box 6339, Honolulu, Hawaii 96818
Telephone: 808-455-1600

CIVIL WAR SOLDIERS MUSEUM
108 South Palafox Place, Pensacola, Florida 32501
Website: http://cwmuseum.org/
E-mail: info@cwmuseum.org
Telephone: 850-469-1900
Fax: 850-469-9328

GETTYSBURG MUSEUM OF THE CIVIL WAR
Visitor Center, Gettysburg National Military Park, 97 Taneytown Road, Gettysburg, PA 17325
Telephone: 717-334-1124

THE LINCOLN ROOM MUSEUM
12 Lincoln Square, Gettysburg, PA 17325
Telephone: 717-334-8188

MILITARY VEHICLE MUSEUM
1918 North Rosemead Boulevard, South El Monte, California
E-mail: tankland@aol.com
Telephone: 626-442-1776 *Fax:* 626-443-1776

THE MUSEUM OF THE CONFEDERACY
1201 East Clay Street, Richmond, Virginia 23219
Website: www.moc.org
Telephone: 804-869-861

NATIONAL MUSEUM OF CIVIL WAR MEDICINE
P.O. Box 470, Frederick, Maryland 21705
Website: www.civilwarmed.org
E-mail: museum@civilwarmed.org
Telephone: 301-695-1864
Fax: 301-695-6823

U.S.S. BOWFIN SUBMARINE MUSEUM AND PARK
11 Arizona Memorial Drive, Honolulu, Hawaii 96818
Telephone: 808-423-1341

INDEX

CREDITS

Pictures researched by Tim Newark.

Special thanks to Peter Newark's Military Pictures for providing the historical illustrations.

Thanks to the following photographers for supplying pictures: Ed Skelding (pages 131, 136, 137); Alec Hasenson (pages 14, 16, 18, 20–21); Ian Knight (pages 122, 126, 128–9); and Kieran Lynch (pages 146, 148–9, 152–3).

Pictures also supplied by Pictor and Pictures Colour Library (pages 138, 145).

All other photographs and illustrations are the copyright of Quarto Publishing plc.

Quarto Publishing would like to thank Ian Howes for the photography of Europe's battlefields.

The author, Tim Newark, would like to thank Philipp Elliot-Wright, Ron Field, and Peter Gascoyne Lockwood.